PRACTICAL ASTROLOGY

BEING A
SIMPLE METHOD OF INSTRUCTION IN
THE SCIENCE OF ASTROLOGY

BY

ALAN LEO

LATE EDITOR OF " MODERN ASTROLOGY "

THIRD EDITION

LONDON
"MODERN ASTROLOGY" OFFICE
IMPERIAL BUILDINGS, LUDGATE CIRCUS, E.C.

The Trade supplied by
L. N FOWLER & Co., 7, IMPERIAL ARCADE, LONDON E.C.

1924

Printed in Great Britain by
Fox, Jones & Co., Kemp Hall Press, High Street, Oxford.

PREFACE

IN issuing this work I have only one motive—which alone has induced me to spare no pains to make my subject as simple and as plain of understanding as possible to those who may never before have heard of planetary influence. And that is, the desire to place the science of Astrology before the world in its true light as a Science, and indeed a Religion too, and not as a jumble of fortune-telling trash. The time has come when the Chaldean and Assyrian religions shall be once more revealed, and the truth with regard to our destiny, as told by the stars, unfolded.

The Wisdom Religion has now in the west taken firm root among those who have thrown off the heavy chains of conventionality, and its leaders by their force of reason and purity of life have now the power to turn the tide of evolution into the channels of progress and liberty. But their theories of fate and freewill, and of the law of action and reaction, need the practical demonstration of this law through the aid of Astrology. I am deeply indebted to certain members of the Theosophical Society, whose untiring efforts and unselfish labours have done far more towards the world's salvation than the present race can as yet appreciate. At their fountain I have drunk of the living waters of TRUTH, and in these pages I have humbly tried to impart some of that truth. Nothing, however, is advanced in this work that has not received the author's careful investigation, personal experience giving weight to each assertion; hence it has at least the merit of originality.

The rules here given will enable the reader by a little practice to commence unravelling the great mystery of life, and as progress is made it will be found that the inequalities of the human race no longer present the great problem that must ever face those who refuse to study the metaphysical, where alone can be found the abstract *cause* for the concrete *event*.

If this book serves no other purpose it will at least help the student to understand HIMSELF, and will throw light upon that verse in *The Light of Asia* which says " . . . ye suffer from yourselves."

One last word. In such a work as this it is impossible to dispense with a free and uncommon use of metaphor, allegory, and analogy. In passing rapidly from one type of imagery to another, many instances of what will at a first glance strike the literary reader as "mixed metaphor" may occur. These it is hoped he will condone as being inevitable under the circumstances.

ALAN LEO.

[*In this New Edition the work remains in substantially the same form as before, though carefully revised and in many details improved; for instance, all tabular matter has been presented in a more concise and convenient form.—A. L.*]

CONTENTS

CONTENTS

INTRODUCTION

THIS work contains "the message of the stars," which is the true meaning of the word Astrology. Through its pages is made the first attempt in modern times to blend the cause with the effect, though it may perhaps be a little premature, as the world's mental atmosphere is yet darkened by preconceived notions, and the playthings that interest the majority have not as yet been placed on one side. But there are nevertheless a few souls ready, and to serve them I have given the best years of my life, so that a foundation may be established upon which to raise above the narrow limitations of prejudice and incompetent criticism the splendid structure of truth.

All I ask from those who are still bound by the conventional fear of public "opinion" is, that they will refrain from condemnation until they *understand* the subject upon which the work treats; and then I hope their candour will allow of their speaking in accordance with the facts, even though these should conflict with preconceived notions. It is unfortunate that there should be so much misunderstanding with regard to the science, but owing to its very nature it demands a highly organised brain and a metaphysical trend of thought to grasp its true significance. This has caused many to regard Astrology as no more than a juggler's method of divination, solely devoted to fortune-telling. Nothing could be farther from the truth, for indeed this science is none other than The Law Which Governs Our Solar System.

The claims here made are either substantially true, or they are false. It is the aim of this book to place before the conscientious inquirer the means of deciding which. To those who are unable to see the supreme significance of even the *possible* truth of this science, it has nothing to say. For them, at present, Astrology has no message.

In these pages will be found the essence of the true Astrology, and the rules given will be found simple, and such as can be readily tested by any intelligent person who is unbiassed enough to make the investigation.

The origin of Astrology is lost in the mists of antiquity. It is the soul of astronomy, and, freed from all the rubbish that has become associated with it, stands as the most practical and scientific exposition of Fate and Destiny the world has ever known. During the coming centuries, while the Sun in his precessional cycle progresses through the sign (or rather constellation) Aquarius, it is destined to become the religion of the race. When the Sun entered Pisces, the sign of the fishes, there came the Saviour Jesus, whose twelve disciples were fishermen, He Himself being born of the virgin sign Virgo, opposite to Pisces. The previous (Jewish) dispensation was that of Aries, the ram; preceded, in Egypt and Assyria, by that of Taurus, the bull.

In this way may be traced the whole past history of the world. Its evolution must now be unfolded through Aquarius, the sign of the MAN, who will soon arise, his mission being to prepare the way for the age of perfected manhood in whom the God may dwell.   In the crystallized religion of the crucified Saviour, who has now risen, we have seen the swelling of the emotions, and through the perfection of the mind His metaphysical second coming may be discerned.

Herein is wisdom.   It is written in the skies that he who runs may read.

THE SIGNS OF THE ZODIAC

Name.	Symbol.	Meaning.
ARIES	♈	The Ram
TAURUS	♉	The Bull
GEMINI	♊	The Twins
CANCER	♋	The Crab
LEO	♌	The Lion
VIRGO	♍	The Virgin
LIBRA	♎	The Balance
SCORPIO	♏	The Scorpion
SAGITTARIUS	♐	The Archer
CAPRICORN	♑	The Goat
AQUARIUS	♒	The Waterman
PISCES	♓	The Fishes

Northern.

Southern.

OLD DOGGEREL RHYME.

The Ram, the Bull, the Heavenly
Twins,
The Crab, and next the Lion
shines
The Virgin, and the Scales ;
The Scorpion, Archer, then Sea-
Goat,
The Man that holds the Water-
ing Pot,
The Fish with glittering tails.

CHAPTER I

THE SIGNS OF THE ZODIAC

THE alphabet of Astrology consists of the twelve signs of the zodiac, which follow each other in order, Aries being the first. The Sun enters Aries on the 21st of March in each year, this being the commencement of the astronomical and astrological year, and continues therein until the 21st of April, when the sign Taurus is reached; and so on, throughout the circle.

THE PLANETARY SYMBOLS ARE:—

Symbol.	Name.	Symbol.	Name.	Symbol.	Name.	Symbol.	Name.
⊙	Sun	♀	Venus	♄	Saturn	⊕	Pars Fortunæ
☽	Moon	♂	Mars	♅	Uranus	☊	Dragon's Head
☿	Mercury	♃	Jupiter	♆	Neptune	☋	Dragon's Tail

THE ASPECTS ARE:—

☌ Conjunction	□ Square	⊡ Sesqui-quadrate	✳ Sextile
☍ Opposition	△ Trine	∠ Semisquare	⊻ Semi-sextile

Par. : Parallel.　Asc. indicates the Ascendant.　M.C. : Midheaven.

Each of the twelve signs contain thirty of the 360 degrees of the circle, the first 30° (that is, from 0° to 30°) being called Aries, the next Taurus, and so on. The first six signs are called Northern, the remainder Southern, as follows:—

Northern Signs.			Southern Signs.		
0° to 30°	♈	Aries	180° to 210°	♎	Libra
30 to 60	♉	Taurus	210 to 240	♏	Scorpio
60 to 90	♊	Gemini	240 to 270	♐	Sagittarius
90 to 120	♋	Cancer	270 to 300	♑	Capricorn
120 to 150	♌	Leo	300 to 330	♒	Aquarius
150 to 180	♍	Virgo	330 to 360	♓	Pisces

These signs are divided (1) into four groups of three

signs each, representing the four great conditions—Spiritual, Mental, Emotional, and Physical; shown also in the four "elements," Air, Fire, Water, and Earth. Thus—

FIERY—Aries, Leo, Sagittarius .   ♈ ♌ ♐
EARTHY—Taurus, Virgo, Capricorn . ♉ ♍ ♑
AIRY—Gemini, Libra, Aquarius . . ♊ ♎ ♒
WATERY—Cancer, Scorpio, Pisces . . ♋ ♏ ♓

It will be seen that from Aries to Pisces they follow in the order of *Fire, Earth, Air*, and *Water* (the virtue of each sign remaining always as given above), and it is therefore important that the student should memorize the signs and their nature thoroughly.

Now (2), there is still another division to be made, viz. into CARDINAL, FIXED, and MUTABLE* Signs. The CARDINAL Signs mark the commencement of the seasons of spring, summer, autumn, and winter, and are composed of Aries (fire), Cancer (water), Libra (air), and Capricorn (earth). The FIXED Signs similarly mark the centre of the seasons, being Taurus (earth), Leo (fire), Scorpio (water), and Aquarius (air). The remaining four must then be the MUTABLE Signs, *i.e.* Gemini, Virgo, Sagittarius, and Pisces, and they mark the end of the seasons. The following illustration will make this clear :—

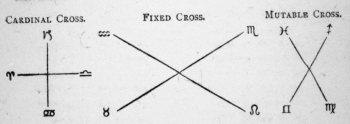

CARDINAL CROSS.   FIXED CROSS.   MUTABLE CROSS.

* Often called "Common" or "flexed" Signs.

These positions should be studied till they become as familiar as the figures on the face of a clock. If this be done, the reader will have little difficulty in understanding the lessons that follow. The accompanying diagram will prove very useful in this study.

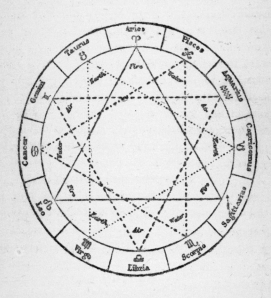

CHAPTER II

THE most essential part of Astrology consists of a thorough knowledge of the Planets and their natures. Taken separately, they may be considered as being, as it were, *individualized parts* of the whole twelve signs of the zodiac, each representing in itself one principle. The Zodiac may be likened to a great band or circle, representing the circumference of the universe, and containing within itself the essence of life—Spirit. Similarly, the Sun may be considered as containing within itself the essence of the planets; for the planets in themselves merely furnish the media through which certain forces act.

The Zodiac, then, may be thought of as a circle surrounding an inner circle, the Sun; the former representing the casket, the latter the jewel. Just so is it with our physical form : *it* is not the man, but merely that which contains the man. A correct understanding of this will give a clear idea of the relation between the Signs of the Zodiac and the Planets (collectively represented by the Sun).

☉   THE SUN   ☉

The symbol of the Sun is a perfect circle with a point in the centre. It is this point which represents the potential essence of everything in nature. We are told in the Wisdom

Religion that "Desire first arose in IT, which was the primal germ of mind," or in Holy Scripture, "In the beginning was the Word, and the Word was with God, and the Word was God" (John i. 1). Now, it was this IT, Word, or "Logos," that was the creative energy, and from it, through *desire*, radiates that which is to be the manifested universe: in Astrology this is symbolized by the dot in the centre of the circle. It is only by *symbology* that we can think out the Divine Creation, and it is the planetary system which best conveys the idea. In order to "know himself," God has to become manifest, and WE are, *in essence*, that God. Until we realize this grand truth, we remain blind, refusing to know ourselves and rejecting God.

In dealing with this great subject, we have no words with which to convey the grandeur of this becoming. During time inconceivable the unmanifest has been manifesting, and only when manifestation is complete shall we recognize our origin. Nevertheless, through that unwritten law which is set in the sky, we may by symbology faintly trace the progress of the infinite to the finite, and thence back to infinitude again. This pilgrimage WE have to make. From God, the infinite, we come, and to God, the infinite, we must return, taking with us the self-conscious realization of ourselves and of the universe which we have gained in our experience with the finite, our "descent into matter."

THE UNFOLDING

Let us consider the evolution, as it were, of the point within the circle, when desire has energized its movement. First, a ray will shoot straight out in one direction, forming the horizontal line, and another in a transverse direction,

forming the vertical, the two together constituting the four
"angles," or angels, thus

equivalent to the four elements, fire—air, and earth—water.
Let us imagine the first or horizontal line to represent the
positive, electric, or *male* element, and the second or vertical
line to typify a reflection of this as the negative, passive, or
female element.   We may carry our idea a little farther,
and imagine this positive ray splitting or expanding the
circle into two halves, thus

We shall thus have evolved two half-circles, and the cross
separated from the circle, giving us, with the original circle,
these three factors

which, for distinction, we may term respectively *spirit, soul,*
and *body*, or Sun, Moon, and Earth.

In the circle we have spirit *absolute;* in the half-circle,
spirit *formative;* and in the cross, spirit *latent;* thus spirit
crystallizes into matter.

Imperfect as this symbology necessarily is, within it lies
the true presentment of involution and evolution.   And
at the back of all religions lies this truth,—the "three-in-
one," Father, Mother, Son; the Sun being the father, the
Moon the mother, and the Earth the child.   Later on we
shall see how beautifully this idea works out.

Now let us for a moment consider the real value of these three symbols, and treat them in their metaphysical aspect. We shall then have *construction*, *preservation*, and *disintegration*,—the Circle (○) as builder of new forms, the Half-Circle (☽) as preserver, and the Cross (+) as destroyer. We shall by this means obtain a true knowledge of the natures of the various planets. For all life is a combination of building up and pulling down : Nature wastes nothing, for it is the purpose of divine economy to reconstruct the new out of the old; and if we were not blind, we should ever perceive this wonderful working of Nature toward perfection.

The foregoing paragraphs are of the utmost importance, for upon the clear understanding of these three principles depends our hope of becoming true astrologers.

Let us proceed to construct the various planets out of our three factors ⊙, ☽, and +.

♂ MARS ♂

We will first place the cross above the circle (thus, ♂), and this will produce the symbol of the planet Mars, the synthesis of all that which is called *desire*; in it is all energy and force, for beneath the cross is the circle—spirit—pushing on toward manifestation, producing Experience, the supreme teacher. In him is *con*struction and *de*struction; for the negative is exalted over the positive, form is paramount over idea, and matter triumphs over spirit, and the negative (+) is illusive to the real and positive (○). The symbol of Mars will therefore represent to us Desire, Force, and Energy.

♀ VENUS ♀

Now let us place the cross under the circle (thus, ♀), when we shall have a true symbol of the planet Venus, the symbol of *love*. Here the circle has surmounted the cross; spirit has forced its way through matter, and it has become one with itself. Until love has entered our hearts, we are not in touch with anything in nature; for Love alone produces harmony, and only by vibrating in harmony with other souls can we come into contact with them, and so know them in the only true sense. And the same is equally true of inanimate objects or "things." In contradistinction to Mars, who is the planet of discord, typifying the animal, Venus represents the human soul, and until we feel the sweet influence of Venus in our lives, we shall go on seeking fresh experience upon the cross of life. Venus is love, while Mars is passion; Venus peace, Mars strife. In her highest aspect Venus is *pure love*, having no desire for self: Mars in his highest aspect is *strength*, protecting the weak. These two planets in themselves are helpful each to the other; but when *abused*, either, or both in co-operation, may become the vilest curse.

☉ THE SUN OR CIRCLE ☉

The Sun may be said to represent these two planets combined, and therefore stands as Power, being Love and Will united. This is the immortal or divine spark in man, and rules the vital principle, being hence the essence of life. We are bathed in this everlasting sun-life while we breathe; and when the solar rays cease to focus themselves in the vital organ, we perforce must change our condition of existence, or "die." The Sun is thus said to rule the life of the individual.

The Sun is the most important of all the planets, for he rules not only our vital energy, but is the medium through which our moral character is denoted, for we must be moral before we can be wise. Therefore the Sun is *power*.

☽   The Moon or Half-circle   ☽

We have thus completed the symbols connected with the cross and circle, representing the spiritual side of our nature. We will now concern ourselves with the mind, or as it is termed by the religious world, the Soul,—the link, as it were, between spirit or *life* and matter or *vehicle*. This will be symbolized by the half-circle, or the magnetic Moon (☽); having two sides, or two halves, she is dual in her nature, constituting what we may term "animal soul" or "vehicle of desire" on the one hand, and mind pure and simple on the other, in accordance with her position and aspects. In her we have the synthesis of the *Psychical World*, and she is the chief factor in Astrology, so that everything relating to her must have special attention; for the mind is a most important part of man.

♄   Saturn   ♄

Now let us place the cross over the half-circle (thus, ♄), and we shall have the planet Saturn, or Satan—the tempter or *tester*. Here we have matter set over mind, representing the cold, dry, and calculating intellect; not true reason, but simply brain-intellect, abundant instances of which may be found in the horoscopes of those "critics" who pretend to pass judgment upon what they do not understand. Saturn is the great planet of "limitation," and is therefore the

centralizing of self, the creator of the Personality. Every
one must pass Saturn before they can distinguish truth from
illusion : his mission is redemption, but his abuse is the extreme of *selfishness*.   He is called the greatest evil because
his experiences are bitter lessons of trial and patience, but
he is the planet of justice—justice absolute and impartial.
None may pass him who have not been weighed in the
balance of the seventh sign.

♃   JUPITER   ♃

If we place the half-circle over the cross (thus, ♃), we
shall produce the planetary symbol of Jupiter. Here mind
has risen over matter, and compassion is the result. The
mind, or soul, has passed upward through experience and
profited by the trials and temptations ; it knows the secret
of life ; it has conquered matter and is free ; and with divine
compassion it feels for struggling humanity. To be filled
with the influence of Jupiter is to know the value of mercy,
and to taste the divine. To be true to Jupiter we must
foster compassion ; we are false when we turn his influence
into personal gain. The religious spirit, that is to say, the
true religious spirit, comes from Jupiter ; it abuses none of
those who are struggling, however imperfectly, upward, but
lends a helping hand to all.

☿   MERCURY   ☿

Having thus formed six planets, ☉ (Sun), ♂ (Mars),
♀ (Venus) ; ☽ (Moon), ♄ (Saturn), ♃ (Jupiter), we have yet
another to complete the seventh, and that is made up of

the three factors combined—half-circle over circle, and circle over cross, thus ☿, the symbol of Mercury, who has been styled "the winged messenger of the gods." It is the planet ♀ who has donned wings and is now able to soar into unknown regions; it has added to its experience that of the manifested self, and has, moreover, extended its help to other selves: in essence, it is wisdom or perfected manhood.

It is the synthesis of all the planets within the manifested universe, being essentially the planet of thought and reason: true talent and skill is represented by this planet, while upon it our judgment depends. Wise men ridicule nothing they cannot understand; but fools boast of their so-called intellect, and pretend that all that they do not know is rubbish and beneath their superior notice.

He who rules his planets, and not the fool who obeys them, is the true son of Mercury. Foolish men do not trouble to concern themselves whether or not the stars rule them, for their time has not come to escape the planetary influence; therefore they go blundering on until some day the teacher Experience causes them to seek for causes: it is then that Mercury lights the lamp of reason, and thenceforward all goes well. But not until the lesson has been learnt will idle men seek to know how much free will they have to combat that which, for them, *is* fate.

The following diagram will to some extent explain the foregoing remarks, and help to make the new method of instruction easy to be understood; after which we will consider the various combinations called aspects.

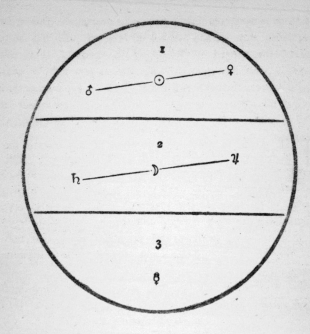

THE NATURE OF THE PLANETS

Principle.	Planet.	Attribute.	
Central Essence	☉	POWER	SUBJECT
Instinctual Consciousness	☽	COLLECTOR	LENS
Immortal Mirror	☿	ILLUMINATOR	MIRROR
Human Soul	♀	LOVE; also WISDOM	BACKGROUND
Energies	♂	DESIRE	FOREGROUND
Permanent Individuality	♃	COMPASSION	LIGHT
Reaper	♄	LIMITATION, or FATE	SHADOW

The planets Uranus and Neptune are specially dealt with in later works.*

* See *How to Judge a Nativity, Part II.*

CHAPTER III

THE ASPECTS

THE puzzle to every student when he has erected the map is to compute the aspects. In reality it is a very simple matter when we know the relationship one set of signs bears to another. If the student has mastered the nature of the signs, and knows *at sight* which are the Fiery, Earthy, Airy, and Watery, then all that is necessary is that he should understand in what aspect they behold each other. The following should be carefully memorized :—

The whole circle of 360° is divided into various parts, each being a simple fraction of the whole, and each constituting in itself an "aspect." To these the following names are given :—

30° Semi-sextile	$\frac{1}{12}$ circle	. .	⋎
45° Semi-square or Semi-quadrate	$\frac{1}{8}$,,	. .	∠
60° Sextile	$\frac{1}{6}$,,	. .	✳
90° Square or Quadrate . .	$\frac{1}{4}$,,	. .	□
120° Trine	$\frac{1}{3}$,,	. .	△
135° Sesqui-quadrate . . .	$\frac{3}{8}$,,	. .	⬓
150° Inconjunct or Quincunx .	$\frac{5}{12}$,,	. .	⚻
180° Opposition	$\frac{1}{2}$,,	. .	☍

The Conjunction occurs when two planets are in the same degree of a sign, or "within orbs," that is, within seven degrees of each other; the opposition when planets are in the same number of degrees in opposite signs. Strictly speaking, these are positions and not aspects. The same may be said of the parallel of declination (par. dec.), which applies to the position of two planets in the same degree of declination North or South of the celestial Equator.

The FIERY signs are always in *trine* aspect to each other, that is, 120° apart. Aries is a fiery sign, and is, therefore, in trine aspect to either Leo or Sagittarius, these three signs being 120° apart.

Starting again from Aries, which is also a Cardinal sign, we find that all the CARDINAL signs are either in *square* aspect or in *opposition* to each other, that is, 90° (or 180°) apart; thus Aries is in square aspect to Cancer and to Capricorn, but in opposition to Libra.

Taurus, which is an earthy sign, is in trine aspect (120°) to the other earthy signs, Virgo and Capricorn. But as a fixed sign Taurus is in square aspect (90°) to Aquarius and Leo, and in opposition to Scorpio.

The next sign in order is Gemini, an airy sign, the first point of which is 60° from the first point of Aries. It is in trine aspect to the airy signs Libra and Aquarius, and as a common sign it is in square aspect with the common signs Virgo and Pisces, and in opposition to Sagittarius. Next is the watery sign Cancer, the second of the Cardinal signs. As a watery sign it is in trine aspect to Scorpio and Pisces, and as a Cardinal sign it is in square aspect to Aries and Libra, and in opposition to Capricorn; and so on with the others.

The following will help the memory :—

Fiery		Fiery signs
Earthy	signs are in trine apect to	Earthy ,,
Watery		Watery ,,
Cardinal		Cardinal signs
Fixed	signs are in square (or opposition) aspect to	Fixed ,,
Common		Common ,,

Any point of the Circle may be taken as a starting point when considering the aspects. For instance, from the fifth degree of Cancer to the fifth degree of Libra is a square aspect; carried to the fifth degree of Scorpio it would be a trine aspect.

When judging of the value of aspects the "application" and "separation" should be noticed. The Moon is the swiftest traveller, and applies to all the planets. If, at birth, she were placed in the fifteenth degree of Aries, she would "apply" to the sextile of a planet in the sixteenth degree of Gemini; to the square of a planet placed in the eighteenth degree of Cancer; to the trine of a planet in the seventeenth degree of Leo, and the opposition of a planet in more than fifteen degrees of Libra. If the planets in these signs were *less* than 15°, then she would be "separating" from the said aspects.

Next to the Moon, Mercury is the quickest traveller of the planets; Venus comes next, then Mars, followed by the Sun, Jupiter, and Saturn, in the order named, each applying to aspects of the other in the above sequence; thus, ☽ ☿ ♀ ☉ ♂ ♃ ♄.

The "orbs," or distances within which the planets act upon each other, are from 5° to 7° either side of the aspect. If we consider the Moon in 15° of Aries, and any planets in Leo from 8° to 22°, the Moon will be applying to or separating from the trine aspect, according to her position in the sign. It is not wise to allow more than 7° as the sphere of influence in which a sextile, square, trine, or opposition will act. The conjunction will also act within seven degrees either side, becoming more complete as the planets approach each other. In dealing with the semi-square or sesqui-quadrate, not more than 3° should be allowed for the sphere of influence.

(There are also "mundane" aspects, arising out of the houses * in which the planets may be, a planet in any part of the first house being in square to one in the *same part* of the fourth or tenth houses, and similarly in opposition to one in the seventh; and so on, just as with the signs, a planet in any degree of Cancer being in square aspect to a planet in or near the same degree of Aries or Libra, &c. These "mundane" aspects, however, are not as a rule much regarded, and they require some calculation to determine accurately.)

The computation of aspects is a matter of practice only, and requires merely a little patience and study; in a short while it becomes as easy as reading the time by a clock. It is absolutely necessary that they should be carefully calculated and correctly judged, and the power of the planets blended, so that the "sentences" of the horoscope, so to speak, may be put together grammatically and logically.

The following method shows planets in aspect at a glance :—

1. Start with the Sun, and see if any other planet is in or near the same degree of another sign—if so, note it.

2. Add to the Sun's position 15° (or subtract 15° if nearer the end of a sign than the beginning), and see if any other planet is in or near *that* degree of another sign—if so, note it.

3. Any planet not fulfilling either of these conditions cannot be in any aspect (except conjunction) with the Sun.

4. Apply the same test to each of the planets, taking them in the following order : ☽ ☿ ♀ ♂ ♃ ♄ ♅ ♆ .

Planets so found are not *all* in aspect, it should be noted, since distances of 15°, 75°, and 105° are also

* See Chapter IX.

shown, and these must be rejected; but by following this course no aspects will be *overlooked*, and that is of most importance.

The diagram appended will help the student to judge how the aspects are formed :—

THE DIVISIONS OF THE CIRCLE

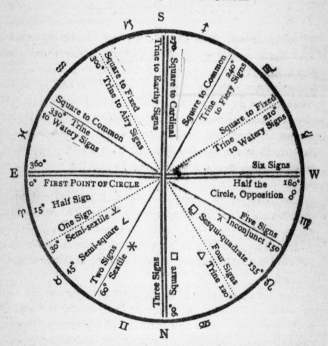

NOTE.—The aspects shown in this diagram, *e.g.* ∠, ✳, ▢, &c., are reckoned, for convenience, from the FIRST point of the circle. But it is the *distance*, of course, which constitutes the aspect, and not the part of the circle or zodiac where it falls. Thus, for example, ♈ 12° is ∠ ♉ 27°, ▢ ♋ 12°, ⊡ ♌ 27°, ⊼ ♍ 12°; similarly, ♉ 5° is △ ♍ 5°; and so on.

CHAPTER IV

THE VALUE OF THE ASPECTS

EACH aspect, from the conjunction to the opposition, has a special value of its own, the whole forming an illustration of the emergence from Unity to Duality. The CONJUNCTION signifies Unity. When Venus and Mars, for instance, are in conjunction, the soul and the senses are one; and complete unity of feeling, acting through the sheath or sign in which the conjunction occurs, is the result. In Napoleon's horoscope the Sun and Mars are in conjunction. Here will and desire are one, and he has the will to carry out his desires.

The next aspect is the SEMI-SEXTILE, or 30° distant, a combination of positive and negative in action, constituting harmony of a very weak order, corresponding to ♈-♉, or ♉-♊. The next is also a weak aspect, the SEMI-SQUARE, 45°; but this is discordant, being half of the square or angular position.

The SEXTILE comes next, corresponding to ♈-♊, or ♉-♋. This is a good aspect, because fire and air are in harmony, and water and earth are in harmony; therefore, there is much sympathy in this aspect, which is not only harmonious, but also well suited to expression on the physical plane.

The SQUARE aspect of 90° is considered very evil, owing to the discord arising from the sharp angles of the cross: it indicates conflict or acute disturbance. For instance, take

the square from Aries to Cancer. Here we have fire and
water, two elements which can never agree; and as all
squares are similarly conflicts between the elements, they
must be evil. Water has nothing in common with fire,
neither has earth sympathy with air: the elements of these
do not, therefore, mix or blend harmoniously, and so a

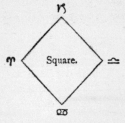

struggle between the two is the result. This is why the
square is called the angle of sorrow. To judge the nature
of the square the principles or planets in conflict must be
noted, as also the sheath through which they are acting.

The next aspect is the TRINE,—always considered good.
Let us see why. Fire agrees with fire, and water with water,
so we judge from the sympathy between the elements forming the trine aspects that harmony results. This is why the
trine is considered the angle of joy. Note the nature of
the trine: in unity there is duality; in duality, unity :—

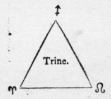

The SESQUI-QUADRATE (135°) and INCONJUNCT (150°)
aspects are weak, the former evil, the latter good or evil, in
accordance with the planets.

The OPPOSITION decidedly manifests duality, and, in a measure, may be considered as evil. Venus in opposition to Mars indicates the struggle between the soul and the senses: they are two, not one; dual, and not unified.

It may be said that the aspects have an influence related to that of the "houses" (Chapter IX.) to which they correspond. Thus the 6th and 8th houses are each distant 150° from the ascendant or starting point; the "inconjunct" aspect has therefore a "6th house" or "8th house" influence, according as the swifter planet applies to or is separating from the opposition of the slower. And so on with the others.

The following table will show at a glance the value of the aspects :—

☌	Conjunction	Unity	*Being*
⚹	Semi-sextile	Resolvent	*Relevancy*
∠	Semi-square	Discordant	*Transition*
✶	Sextile	Harmonious	*Reasonableness*
□	Square	Sorrowful	*Precipitation: crystallization*
△	Trine	Joyous	*Solution: re-solution*
⊡	Sesqui-quadrate	Discordant	*Transmutation*
150° or ⚻	Inconjunct	Circulating	*Trituration: purgation*
☍	Opposition	Dualistic	*Balance: marriage*
P. or Par.	Parallel		(acts as Conjunction or Opposition).

The nature of the aspects should be well studied *in connection with the signs in which they occur.* For instance, ☉ □ ♄ (Sun square Saturn) from Aries to Cancer will have a totally different effect if reversed. When the Sun is in Aries it is in a fiery sign of its own nature, while Saturn is in a cold moist sign, similar to its nature. If Saturn be compared to a solid block of ice when in this sign, the Sun from Aries with its fiery strength will in time melt the ice, and the resultant flood of water may be likened to the emotions which will be stirred by the melting heat of the spirit. Reversing this aspect, Saturn in Aries would make the brain so limited and selfish that the emotions of Cancer could be rarely, if ever, touched. Saturn in Leo square Mars in Taurus would be an exceedingly evil aspect. The limitations of the heart would find expression only through cruel, bitter, and hard speech.

The nature of the planets must be well understood before any of the aspects can be comprehended, the Sun and Jupiter affecting the moral and spiritual nature, the Moon and Saturn the mind and personal nature. All evil is the abuse of good, for good and evil are but the "pairs of opposites," and behind both is the one eternal, never-changing Real Self. The aspects indicate the path we tread until we overcome what is called evil, and use the good to understand God and His manifestations.

The planets aspecting each other affect certain *principles* or qualities. By knowing the natures of the planets we can judge what effect the aspects they hold to each other will have upon ourselves. In Chapter II. we explained the planets' natures as follows :—

♂ Desire, passion, strength.
♀ Love, affection, feeling.

♄ Self, limitation, coldness.
♃ Sympathy, compassion, warmth.

☿ Memory, perception, thought.

☽ Personal receiver and collector.
☉ The Individual Centre.

If we blend these aspects we could judge ♂ △ ♀ as desire in harmony with love or feeling. If the aspect were ♂ □ ♀, desire would be in conflict with love. Sun trine

Saturn, self and individuality in harmony; when in square aspect, limitations and sorrows through selfishness. Aspects to Venus affect the feelings; to Mars, the desires; to the Moon, the fate or environment; to Jupiter, the higher spiritual qualities; and so on, as we shall explain further on under the heading of judgment.

CHAPTER V

THE EXALTATIONS OF THE PLANETS

CERTAIN zodiacal signs have been allotted to the various planets as "rulers," in which each has what is termed its *house*, *exaltation*, *fall*, or *detriment*, and every Astrologer must have a complete knowledge of these before he attempts to give a judgment upon nativities. A planet is strong in its *house* or *exaltation*, but weak in its *fall* or *detriment*. The "detriment" is the sign opposite to that which is termed the "house"; and the "fall" the sign opposite to the "exaltation," as will be seen by the following table:—

Ruler.	Exaltation.	Sign.	Fall.	Detriment.
♄	—	♒	—	☉
♃	♀	♓	☿*	☿
♂	☉	♈	♄	♀
♀	☽	♉	—	♂
☿	—	♊	—	♃
☽	♃	♋	♂	♄
☉	—	♌	—	—
☿	☿*	♍	♀	♃
♀	♄	♎	☉	♂
♂	—	♏	☽	♀
♃	—	♐	—	☿
♄	♂	♑	♃	☽

* This is according to general tradition. But there are some thinkers who argue that since ♍ is the *house* of ☿, which is incontestable, it cannot therefore be the *exaltation* also; and hence they assign that dignity to ♒, with which the planet has very great sympathy.

It will be observed that, starting from the ☉ and ☽, the planets range out in either direction, in the order of their relative motion, ☿ first, then ♀, and so on. Planets are the *Lords* or *rulers* of the signs allotted to them as houses, and it is important that students should become thoroughly familiar with these, so that on seeing a horoscope they can at once recognize the lords or rulers of the various houses or signs. Some of the planets, it will be noticed, have two signs, one of these being the positive or "day house," the other the negative or "night house"; that is to say, *by day* the "day house" must be taken as the house, *by night* the "night house."

The following table shows these at a glance :—

PLANET.	Positive or day		Negative or night		HOUSE.
♄					♒
♃					♓
♂	,,	,,			♈
♀			,,	,,	♉
☿	,,	,,			♊
☽	,,	,,	,,	,,	♋
☉	,,	,,	,,	,,	♌
☿			,,	,,	♍
♀	,,	,,			♎
♂			,,	,,	♏
♃	,,	,,			♐
♄			,,	,,	♑

The Sun and Moon have but one house each, Leo and Cancer respectively.

It is now necessary to explain why certain planets should have special signs for their exaltations, and to get a better idea of the reason we must dissect the twelve signs into

four distinct groups, of three signs each, as follows :—
Fiery, Airy, Watery, and Earthy, known as the four
triplicities.

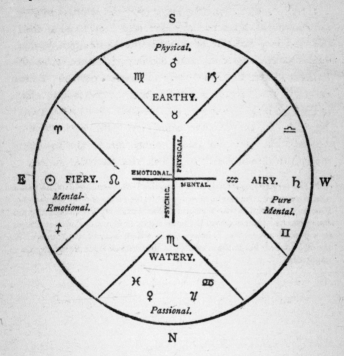

The *fiery* signs ♈ ♌ ♐ we shall class as mental-emotional ;
the *airy* ♊ ♎ ♒ as pure mental ; the *watery* ♋ ♏ ♓ as
psychic and passional ; and the *earthy* ♉ ♍ ♑ as the
physical, intellectual-mental, and practical.

We shall later on, it will be seen, group them as follows :—CARDINAL signs ♈ ♋ ♎ ♑ mental, generally ;
FIXED ♉ ♌ ♏ ♒ vital ; and the COMMON ♊ ♍ ♐ ♓ as

the mutable; but we will now confine our attention to the four, giving the foregoing diagram as illustration to make the explanation easier.*

It will be seen from the above that the strong, energetic, and passional Mars occupies the earthy or physical triad; the life-giving Sun, the fiery and spiritual or eastern portion; while Saturn, the cold and contracting planet, rules the intellect in the mental and airy or western portion. In the centre of the diagram is a solid cross, at the foot of which is the emotional or watery trine, presided over by Venus and Jupiter. To the intuitive mind very little explanation is needed; but there are those whose minds are not quite metaphysical, and for them a little elucidation is added.

---

* The terms "emotional" and "psychic" here employed relate to the positive and negative emotions respectively, the active and the sympathetic, diversely expressed as *true sentiment* and as *sentimentality*. In the diagram here given the planets shown are to be regarded as relating to these stages in a general sense only; they are not, it will be noticed, the "rulers" of the signs shown, but they are exalted in the *cardinal* signs of the respective triplicities.

CHAPTER VI

THE PLANETS AND SIGNS

WE have seen that certain planets have exaltations in special signs, thus giving to each planet three modes of expression, as follows :—

	Planet.		Houses.			Exaltation.
1	♂	♈		♏		♑
2	♀	♉		♎		♓
3	☿	♊		♍		♍
4	♃	♐		♓		♋
5	♄	♑		♒		♎

The Sun and Moon are omitted from the above table for reasons which will soon be quite clear. We have here five planets, corresponding to the five senses,—tasting, or *desire*; feeling, or *touch* (tact); seeing, or *perception*; smelling, or *sympathy*; and hearing, or *contemplation*, respectively.

But we have a "sixth" sense forcing itself into evidence, and for this also we must find a symbol and a house. This is "intuition" or "inspiration," * the symbol for which must be ♅ Uranus, as the following will show. The Sun has but one house, ♌, the opposite sign to which is ♒, into which we must place ♅ as ruler, for this reason. We have

* Intuition is the more correct word for this faculty, signifying the being *taught within*; in "inspiration," properly so called, the inspired person does not himself realize the greatness of his utterances.

three great states of being, the *physical*, *mental*, and *spiritual*, marked off in this manner :—The Physical in its highest form of manifestation is represented by Mercury, the child of the Sun and Moon ; the psychic, or lower Mental, is represented by the maternal condition or the Moon, and therefore precedes every physical change of state ; and lastly, the Spiritual is represented by the Sun, which marks off that which is to be, all future manifestation taking place first in the spiritual realms.

The future of every existing condition is denoted by the opposite sign to its present manifestation, as follows :—

MINOR EVOLUTION.

♂ ♈   Destruction | Adjustment, peace   ♎ ♀

MAJOR EVOLUTION.

☉ ♌   Construction | Perfection   ♒ ♅

It is this Uranian influence which is now pouring in and disturbing the minds of those who had lapsed into the illusive conception of social equality, and it is this influence that will produce the forthcoming social revolution which must precede the birth of the new era which we are now awaiting. The influence of ♅ may be well expressed by the word TRANSLATION.

If we refer to the table of the planets at the commencement of this chapter, it will be seen that ☿ precedes and follows ☉ and ☽, and is housed in ♍, the opposite of which is ♓, or the house of Neptune ♆, the symbol of the "seventh sense," if it may be so called. This influence is only just making itself apparent, but it may be well expressed by the word TRANSMUTATION.

It will be difficult for any but the Uranian mind to follow this symbology, so we shall only return to it by gradual

reference as opportunity offers of making ourselves clear.
But those taking up the study of Astrology must before all
things free their minds from prejudice and be ever prepared
for *new ideas*, such as we hope to unfold as these lessons
advance.

With regard to the "exaltations," it will be found that
the majority occur upon the *cardinal* cross, the symbol of
the head. If we now refer to our three crosses given in
Chapter I., we shall have the exaltations taking the following form :—

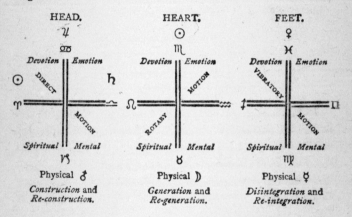

With the first cross we shall find a perfect conflict—Mars,
desire and passion, opposed to Jupiter, compassion, and
Sun opposed to Saturn. But what is the inner meaning?
Mars has become subdued, and is at home in the house of
Saturn; he issued forth as hot and impulsive desire, and
through many experiences he has reached the tenth sign
(the perfect number), and has become purified by his contact with matter and Saturn (mind). He can travel no farther
round : he has reached his culminating point, and his force

must either be indrawn into compassion, represented by Jupiter at the top of the cross, or he must wend his way wearily back to the place whence he started.

There is much food for thought in these exaltations, and to the true astrologer this Astro-philosophy has a very deep meaning. For a moment we will consider Saturn *exalted* in ♎. The lower mind, Saturn, has here reached *the Balance*; it may either go on seeking externals, or be indrawn into the Sun or individuality. It is here literally "weighed in the balance." A study of these ideas will lead to the inner meaning of Astrology.

CHAPTER VII

BEFORE attempting to cast the horoscope we must obtain a complete knowledge of the nature of the Twelve Signs of the Zodiac, so that we may not subsequently confuse them with the Twelve Houses of The Heavens. Students are apt to find much confusion in the terms houses and signs, especially as each sign is styled the "house" of some planet. It may be stated here that the Twelve Houses of The Heavens consist of a twelvefold division of the celestial sphere as viewed from any given place at any given moment, say, the moment of birth; and this then constitutes the framework of the horoscope, into which the planets are subsequently inserted in their due places. These twelve divisions correspond with the respective twelve signs. But for the present we are only concerned with the signs alone, and we therefore proceed.

Each sign must be considered as a sheath or body for the planet, as a principle, to function through. We have seen that each planet has two houses, with the exception of the Sun and Moon, thus giving three sides or aspects to one principle, which we may call Light, Primary, and Dark; the light being the day house, or positive expression, the planet itself the primary, and the night house the dark or negative, each forming, as it were, a trine in itself, as follows :—

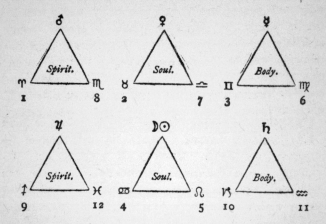

In a similar way each child is born "under" a sign of the zodiac, this being the sign which ascends at birth.

We are the result of the union of two forces in nature, male and female, or positive and negative—being represented by the ☉ and ☽; and if we imagine a line drawn from the Sun to the Moon, the central point of that line will be the critical or sensitive spot at conception, which will find its external expression in the ascendant at birth : it will then be the focusing point between the midheaven or the tenth house and the fourth house, which severally represent the parents. For instance, if ♑ be the culminating sign, then ♋ will be on the fourth house, and the central or mid-way point (♈) will be the ascending sign. This fourth house will symbolize the mother, and the tenth the father, and the ascendant the child. The symbols for the parents, somewhat differently interpretated, will also represent the environment the child is born into. But we will first consider each sign separately, and refer to the above remarks (which should be taken in quite a general sense) at a later period in our studies. The following brief descriptions will for the present enable us to obtain some clue to the nature of each sign, but a fuller and more complete description will be found in *Astrology for All*, where the nature of each sign is described in great detail.

♈ ARIES ♈
(The Sheath of Mars.*)

⊙ *enters* ♈ *March* 21.

The first sign of the zodiac is the *Cardinal*, (movable or changeable) and *Fiery* sign ARIES—the Ram. This is the point from which all astrological calculations are reckoned. It rules the *head*, and is the sign of the ram, from which we obtain our R. A. M. or Right Ascension of the Meridian. The Sun enters this sign about the 21st of March each year.

Each sign is also in itself a trinity, just as we have shown each planet and its two houses to be, being composed of Light, Primary, and Dark, being divided into three "decanates" or spaces of 10° each,—the first ten degrees † being called the first "decanate"; from 10° to 20° the second; and from 20° to 30° the third. The first decanate always partakes of the nature of the sign itself; the next is of the nature of the next sign of the same triplicity—of the same *nature*, that is to say, fiery, earthy, airy, or watery

---

* The expression "sheath" is here used to convey the idea that Aries is the sign through which Mars can most readily find expression.

† *i.e.* from 0° 1' to 9° 59', *inclusive*; and so on.

as the case may be,—while the third decanate is of the nature of the remaining sign of the same triplicity. Thus, the three decanates of Aries are, ♈-♈, ♈-♌, ♈-♐, the influence of ♈ being always the most prominent.

The first or *light* decanate of Aries is therefore of the nature of Mars, since ♂ rules ♈, and this portion of the sign takes upon itself the full and complete nature of Mars in its most external aspect; being the positive portion, it indicates one bold, resolute, and determined. The Sun is exalted in the next decanate, ♈-♌, which is the *primary* portion. It indicates authority and power, and gives strength and justice. The next decanate, ♈-♐, from 20° to 30°, belongs to Jupiter, and being the dark portion of the sign, it indicates threats and undecided action, more inclined to sport than to act.

Taking the sign as a whole, it denotes persons who are ambitious, impulsive, and often irritable, but full of courage and energy, never happy unless they are at the head, or in command of others; they are often generous, but yet selfish enough to study their own ends first; they are very changeable, therefore their passions, if hot while they last, are soon over; they are progressive, and will never quite submit to be governed by others. It is the most positive sign of the zodiac, and gives a very destructive and aggressive spirit. The following is a general description of the bodily characteristics: Spare and strong body, of stature rather above the average; face long; eyebrows bushy; neck long; shoulders thick and powerful; complexion sallow or swarthy; hair black or sandy; disposition irritable. The first half of the sign gives a stronger constitution and a greater muscular development than the latter half. The symbol ♈ indicates the overflow of force from the root, and it always tends to work its way out on the mental plane. These persons have large perceptions, with destructiveness and combativeness fully developed. They are DAUNTLESS.

♉ TAURUS ♉

(The Sheath of Venus.)

⊙ *enters* ♉ *April* 21.

The second sign of the zodiac is TAURUS—the Bull. It governs the *neck* and *throat*. It is the first of the *Fixed* and *Earthy* signs. The first decanate, ♉-♉, is ruled by ♀, and inclines to ease and luxury; it gives some discontent. The central portion from 10° to 20°, ♉-♍, is governed by ☿ : the Moon has her exaltation in the third degree of the preceding decanate, but is also favourable to this portion, in which success in gardening and farming is indicated : it is the best face of the sign. The next decanate, ♉-♑, is ruled by Saturn, and indicates secretiveness and misfortune, and frequently poverty and misery.

The sign Taurus as a whole is unfortunate, and means labour; therefore ♉ persons are generally plodders; they are patient, and will wait for opportunities with apparent indifference,—which as a rule is due to mere stubbornness,— but they are tenacious and self-willed. They can be very industrious and self-reliant, and have splendid memories; they are, however, inclined to be exacting, domineering, and very jealous; they live chiefly in the physical or external world. They are of middle stature, thick and well-set body, and generally have a broad forehead, full face, and prominent eyes; nose and mouth are wide; complexion swarthy; hair dark or black, often curly; disposition placid, indifferent, or sullen, slow to anger, but when provoked furious. The sign is made from the Sun and Moon joined together, thus ♉. Their true quality should be ENDURANCE.

♊ GEMINI ♊
(The Sheath of Mercury.)
⊙ *enters* ♊ *May* 21.

The third sign is GEMINI—the Twins. It is an *Airy* and *Mutable* sign, and governs the *arms, hands, and shoulders*, also *the lungs and nervous system*. The first decanate, ♊-♊, is ruled by ☿; it is the positive portion, and inclines to self-esteem and often hypocrisy. The second, ♊-♀, ruled by ♀, is one of either complaisance or sensuousness. The last, ♊-♒, is profound and contemplative, inclined to science.

Taking Gemini as a whole, it is decidedly dual in its nature, and being the sheath of the convertible planet Mercury, it is a difficult sign to fully understand, being half disposed towards the concrete and practical, and half towards the intellectual or ideal.

Those under its influence are chiefly concerned with intellectual attainments; for this sign lacks what the preceding sign has too much of—affection,—while that is equally short of what this has in over-abundance—intellect. Those governed by this sign are highly observant and generally thoughtful, and are always fond of the arts or sciences; they are very nervous and restless, and often go to extremes, for they are generally suspicious, rarely trusting others, thinking all have the same qualities which they themselves possess, which sometimes include envy and a tendency to "sharp practice": as a rule, they are inclined to be superficial. This sign being the head of the airy triplicity, they are generally very quick and active, but lack continuity, their best qualities being energy, mental activity, and intuition regarding mental or artistic subjects; for they readily apprehend *ideas* and *principles*. They have usually a tall and straight body, dark, sanguine complexion, hair blackish, eyes hazel, sight quick; a smart, active appearance; disposition fickle; understanding good. The symbol of the sign Gemini is made thus ♊, and its distinguishing characteristic is INTELLECT.

♋   CANCER   ♋

(The Sheath of the Moon.)

☉ *enters* ♋ *June* 21.

The fourth sign of the zodiac is the *Watery* and *Cardinal* (changeable) sign CANCER—the Crab. This sign is negative and feminine, being very magnetic and receptive. It presides over the breasts and stomach. The first decanate is ruled by the Moon; it gives many changes, rashness, capability for many foolish acts, and is generally unfortunate. The second decanate is governed by ♂, and signifies one of shrewd methods, with some intuition; it generally indicates successful changes. It is the exaltation of Jupiter. The third decanate, ruled by ♃, indicates sympathy and fecundity, the planet being always fruitful in a moist sign.

Cancer as a whole is a fruitful and sustaining sign. It is the most psychic and occult of the twelve, giving, however, strong leanings toward sensation. Nevertheless, Cancer persons are usually sympathetic and kind, and thoughtful for those who call out their grand maternal principle, though otherwise very apt to be selfish, the instinct for personal aggrandizement being exceptionally strong. Persons born under this sign are very sensitive and very magnetic; their power to draw from others is marvellous, and this makes them very liable to disease. They are reflective and persistent, and generally self-reliant, with yet a strange contradictory tendency to cling to others, this being the sign of "attachment." They have moderate stature, upper part of body somewhat large; small round face, with pale, delicate complexion; brown hair; small gray or light blue eyes; effeminate in constitution and disposition, and subject to chest affections. The symbol of the sign is made of the figures 6 and 9, thus ♋. Its supreme virtue is TENACITY.

♌ LEO ♌

(The Throne of the Sun.)

☉ *enters* ♌ *July* 22.

The fifth sign of the zodiac, LEO—the Lion,—is the central point of the *Fixed* and *Fiery* signs, and represents the Heart of All Things. It rules the *heart* and *back*. Although electric in its outward expression, it is internally the primary central spot, for the heart of all things is Love. It is in this sign we "read the number of the beast." The Moon falls back from Cancer into this sign, in which the personality is swallowed up; and in this sign Saturn falls. The first decanate indicates stability and power; it is the face of steadfast, unswerving action. The second decanate is ruled by Jupiter, and denotes forgiveness and non-resentment of injury. The third is governed by Mars, and indicates organizing ability; it is the most peaceful portion of the whole twelve signs. It is the point where the lion lies down with the lamb, which solves the riddle of the sphinx, for here ♌ joins ♍. Some of these remarks will hardly be understood perhaps, for it is impossible to speak of these things except in symbol or parable; and, unless the intuition catches the hidden meaning, the phrase seems purposeless and nonsensical. But so does any foreign language to one who does not understand it.

The sign as a whole represents the heart, and indicates great self-control. But the love nature of those born under this sign is their weakness; for they are very easily led, being inclined to act according to their feelings, rather than their judgment. Their fine sensitive love nature causes them to be often misunderstood by a sordid and selfish race; for they often live in an ideal world; they are very conscientious, generous,—too generous,—and desire justice and harmony. They have much internal courage, and are very determined, though often impulsive; their power in the world is enormous when opportunity affords. Description:—Large stature, broad shoulders, prominent and large eyes, oval, ruddy countenance; of a high, resolute, haughty, and ambitious temper. (This is the typical ♌ person, but there are some slight and highly sensitive varieties.) The last half of the sign produces a body much shorter and darker than the first. The symbol is formed from the lion's tail, thus ♌. The virtue of this sign is the true COMPASSION, which is the only real Love and the foundation of all permanent Power.

♍ VIRGO ♍

(The Sheath of Mercury.)

☉ *enters* ♍ *August* 22.

The sixth sign of the zodiac, Virgo, is the internal or primary of the earthy triplicity; it is a *Common* and *Earthy* sign, the negative house of Mercury, which planet has great power therein. It governs the *bowels*. This is the sign of the celestial virgin.

The first decanate, ♍-♍, is ruled by ☿, and gives *finesse* and subtlety, and a keen interest in all things intellectual. The second, ♍-♑, is ruled by ♄, and gives a love of chastity, prudence, and imagination of a lofty character. In this decanate is the exaltation of Mercury. The third decanate, ♍-♉, is ruled by ♀, and gives a love of art or learning.

Taken as a whole, Virgo is the next best sign to Leo in the zodiac, Leo being the internal spirit, and Virgo the outward manifestation of that spirit through the virgin or pure mind. All the saviours of the world had this sign for their starting point. It rules the "solar plexus." Generally it gives very fine discriminating power and accurate judgment. The chief point about Virgo persons is their great *internal* purity, though they are often externally the opposite of what the inward nature desires. They are often very hopeful and contented under difficulties, though, being highly critical as well as very conscientious, they sometimes display a tendency to worry. They have always good brains, and are excellent business people, while, with their internal intuition and external reasoning, they are among the most clever of the twelve types, making good speakers, and being in general very practical and exceedingly ingenious. They are usually of middle stature, rather slender, but very neat and compact; they have dark hair and complexion; a high-pitched voice; are witty (though often quite lacking in a sense of *humour*), ingenious, and studious, but of a fickle disposition. The symbol of Virgo is made by writers somewhat like the letter " m " crossed at the end, and is printed thus ♍. The virtue of this sign is purity and CHASTITY.

♎ LIBRA ♎

(The Sheath of Venus.)

☉ *enters* ♎ *September* 22.

The seventh sign, Libra, is a *Cardinal* and *Airy* sign, and governs the *reins* and *kidneys*. The first decanate is governed by ♀, and is considered the face of discretion, wisdom, and justice; it is serious and prudent, and has much to do with graceful elocution. The second decanate is ruled by Saturn, and gives some talent in a business direction, with a tendency to appreciate harmony and a quiet life; it is a profitable portion, often giving success. The third, from 20 degrees to 30 degrees, is governed by ☿, and is sensitive and artistic in its nature. On the whole Libra is an equable sign, as signified by its symbol, the balance.

The Librans are generally modest, unassuming persons, with wonderful intuitions, which they seem to draw from an unseen library of their own, as it were. But they are also peculiarly receptive to the influence of others, and when mixing with people should always take care to maintain a positive attitude until they understand the mind they have to deal with. They are very affectionate and exceptionally demonstrative, but they lack the push and energy necessary to elevate themselves when in uncongenial surroundings. They seek quiet, and love to retire into themselves, where they often find "that rest and peace which the world cannot give"; they should choose a professional life, being totally unfitted for any form of physical labour.

This sign often produces a most beautifully formed body; but this must not be taken to imply that no unprepossessing people are born under it. The first half gives a tall and slender form, the latter half stouter and shorter, also darker; the face is round and lovely, the complexion almost perfect, and the eyes generally blue. The symbol is made of a straight and crooked stick, thus ♎. Libra people are always refined; they usually have very large perceptions, and rarely reason, being led by what may be considered the special characteristic of this sign—INTUITION.

♏ SCORPIO ♏
(The Sheath of Mars.)
⊙ enters ♏ October 23.

This is the eighth sign of the zodiac, a *Watery* and *Fixed* sign. It rules *the secret parts*. The first decanate is of ♂, and signifies courage and generosity. The second decanate is ruled by ♃, and indicates a studious nature and one fond of the arts and sciences. The third is governed by the ☽, and is rather unfortunate, yet has in it much justice; those born under it are generally very honourable and sincere.

Taking Scorpio as a whole, it is one few seem to thoroughly understand. But experience has shown that there are two distinct classes of Scorpio persons; we think, too, this applies to all the fixed signs, as we shall point out later on.

One class may be styled mystics: the other materialists. The latter are often secretive, and have strong passions; are rarely if ever "milk-and-water," being quite decided in their ideas of life; are always inclined to be jealous, though this and nearly all their vices they conceal under large dignity. They are persistent and determined, they are keen though not over-tender in their feelings, and can be very exacting; their temper when aroused is severe, and usually highly resentful. This sign produces the finest doctors and surgeons; they have a natural instinct with regard to the physical organism, and are very magnetic; as herbalists, also, Scorpio people often display remarkable power in healing the sick.

They are not easy to describe, but the following will generally fit them: middle size, well set, very strong and robust; complexion dark or dusky; hair often dark, plentiful, strong and elastic; neck as a rule thick; eyes generally dark and magnetic; person hairy. The symbol is made in the form of a writhing serpent, thus ♏. They are reserved and thoughtful, and have as a rule more self-esteem and approbativeness combined than any other sign; but they have a very strong will, and display the dual attributes of GENERATION and RE-GENERATION.

♐   SAGITTARIUS   ♐

(The Sheath of Jupiter.)

☉ enters ♐ November 22.

The ninth sign is a *Mutable*, double-bodied, and *Fiery* sign, and rules the *thighs*. The first decanate gives religious tendencies and some inclination to covetousness; the second a somewhat changeable nature, not always sincere; and the third a romantic tendency, with some obstinacy and wilfulness.

Taking the sign as a whole, it may be considered of a just and honourable disposition; it gives great activity of mind and body, with a strange prophetic power, and those born under this sign often make true predictions quite unexpectedly. They love everything that is open and free, are kind hearted and very sympathetic, but often far too impulsive, often going to great extremes. They are far-seeing, generous, and sincere, but too quick for the majority of their friends. As described, they are generally well formed, tall, and considered handsome. They have an open countenance, Grecian nose, and always remarkable eyes, being fine, clear, and usually dark brown, though sometimes clear sky-blue. The symbol is made in the shape of an arrow, thus ♐. They are always fond of outdoor exercise, and display activity, sympathy, and INSIGHT.

♑ CAPRICORN ♑
(The Sheath of Saturn.)

☉ *enters* ♑ *December* 21.

The tenth sign of the zodiac is Capricorn, a *Cardinal* and *Earthy* sign, ruling the *knees* and *skin*. The first face of ten degrees is controlled by ♄, and gives steadfastness, sincerity, and discreet action. The second face is ruled by ♀, and inclines to good. The third face is governed by ☿, and gives desire to rule, with political ability. Capricorn is an important sign, and gives authority and power, but it deals chiefly with the external world. Capricorn people are generally deep thinkers and often splendid orators; their most remarkable feature is their desire for intellectual attainments. They can carry out large undertakings better than people of any other sign, being practical and self-reliant; but they are often proud and independent, yet very patient and persistent, returning to the attack of difficulties again and again, in spite of all opposition. They are very magnetic and make excellent teachers, being nearly always calm, cool, and collected. They are not very fond of affectionate demonstrations, but can be very sincere and faithful in their affections. They have a large amount of selfishness in their nature, yet small self-esteem. They are often covered over as it were with a deep crust which is hard to penetrate; but once break through this, and they display a real earnestness. They are usually short and not well formed, have thin beard and dark hair, with a long thin pale face and "scraggy" neck. The symbol is made of V and S, thus ♑. They invariably have a fancy for politics. Their keynote is UNDERSTANDING.

♒ AQUARIUS ♒

(The Sheath of Saturn.)

⊙ *enters* ♒ *January* 20.

This is the eleventh sign, and by nature *Airy* and *Fixed*. It rules the *eyes*, *blood*, and *the ankles*. The first decanate is ruled by ♄, and signifies one not to be fully relied upon; it brings sorrow and trouble. The second is ruled by ☿, and is the decanate of modesty, prudence, and affable, kind disposition. The third face is governed by ♀, and denotes individuality.

This sign is probably the most difficult of any to understand, being a mixture of the two other airy signs Libra and Gemini, possessing all the fine intuitive faculties of Libra, but also much of the external nature of Gemini. Those born under this sign are either very weak or very strong. They are nearly always kind hearted; they make excellent character readers, and have splendid discriminative power. Their internal spiritual nature is remarkable, but they are slow to give it expression, for they seem to need a goad to force them into action, being utterly weak and useless until they have discovered their spiritual strength, when they become capable of great possibilities. They are nervous and very keenly sensitive. Materialism is their ruin; but when awakened to spiritual truth their soul grows quickly. They usually have a middle stature, well set, robust, and strong; a good clear and delicate yet sanguine complexion; hazel eyes and flaxen hair; in fact, they are very good looking, ranging next to Libra for beauty; are fond of the water, and make very faithful friends. The symbol is made of two wavy lines, thus ♒. Their special faculty is a knowledge of HUMAN NATURE.

♓ PISCES ♓
(The Sheath of Jupiter.)
☉ enters ♓ February 19.

The twelfth and last sign of the zodiac is Pisces, a *Watery, Mutable*, and "double" sign: it rules *the feet*. The first decanate is ruled by ♃, and gives good judgment: the second is ruled by the ☽, and gives a strong inclination toward the mystical sciences; the last portion is governed by ♂, and gives high self-esteem and some sorrowful experiences.

This sign is decidedly dual, yet on the whole good, for there is a great deal of the Jupiter nature in it. Pisces people can nearly always be relied upon; they are never fully appreciated, for they will keep their talents in the background in a very unassuming way, being very modest in their pretensions. Yet they are inclined to worry too much, and are even obstinate. They are liable to intellectual folly, which often springs from a gloomy and fore-boding nature, owing to their not being properly understood; they are apt to be inaccurate and careless in speech; they can be very loving and affectionate, are too often restless, over-anxious, and sensitive. As a rule they are not for-tunate persons, and it often happens that they live double lives, either voluntarily or because they are in some way compelled to. Their greatest danger is spiritualism, for, being full of sympathy, they make easy " mediums," and are apt to give themselves entirely up for others, who fre-quently wreck their lives, bringing them sorrow and misery. They need especially more *self-reliance*. They are generally thick-set persons with large, pale and fleshy faces, usually dark hair, large watery eyes, arms and legs short. The symbol, made of two half-circles, thus)(, probably means the binding of two souls, or the blending of the positive and negative elements together, and may thus indicate free-dom from bondage. The planet Venus is exalted in this sign. When self-reliance has been cultivated these persons become very useful members of the human family. They are capable of achieving PEACE.

The general outlines only of the twelve signs have here been sketched, for the purpose of giving the student some idea of their nature : we shall deal with each sign more fully farther on. The nature of the sign in itself has been described, and this will apply more or less to all born within the periods of the year indicated. Practice and experience will enable the student to greatly enlarge upon the hints we have given.

The descriptions will not fit *each* individual born in the particular sign described, except in a general way only,—

for the SUN represents the highest part of our nature, and is therefore often least in evidence, the Rising Sign and the position of the ruling planet and the Moon having a great deal to do with the description, as we shall illustrate later.

The foregoing paragraph is of importance, since, in spite of repeated explanations in text-books distinctly stating that such is not the case, beginners frequently imagine that the characteristics ascribed to the various signs necessarily apply, and apply *only*, to all those born during the corresponding months of the year. This is not so, for in spite of the inner character being very largely influenced by the sign occupied by the Sun, yet other modifying influences, which will be detailed in their due place, may be so strong (or may lie, as it were, so much *nearer the surface*), as almost totally to obscure the said qualities—and even, in some cases, to overlay them with attributes of a quite contrary nature.

This misapprehension has been responsible for more confusion on the part of the public in regard to zodiacal influence than perhaps any other single cause.

Let it be clearly understood, then, that "AN ARIES PERSON," for instance, *is a person who from any cause strongly manifests the* ARIES *nature* (whether by having the Sun, Moon, Rising Sign, Ruling Planet, or a satellitium of planets, in that sign), and *not necessarily any one born between 21st March and 21st April in any year*. Similarly, of course, with regard to all the other signs.

It is perhaps better to caution the reader against this very prevalent error here, than to leave it until a later stage where the discussion of the whole matter more properly belongs.

CHAPTER VIII

THE GROUPINGS OF THE SIGNS

NOT only has each sign of the zodiac a distinct and special value of its own, but each degree of the sign also has a decided and definite meaning, containing in itself the number, colour, and form of the individual.* This is a consideration which up to the present has entirely escaped the attention of the western astrological student. In the foregoing chapter we have faintly specialized each sign, and in the present we will condense the twelve signs into four major groups.

In the book of the Prophet Ezekiel there is mention made of the four great cherubim,—the Bull, the Lion, the Eagle, and the Man,—representing the four fixed or central points of each trinity, familiar to all Astrologers as the signs Taurus, Leo, Scorpio, and Aquarius; these collectively forming the central or "fixed" *cross* of the zodiac, the understanding of which at once makes the whole twelve signs simple and easy of comprehension. Taking each one of these four signs as a central point, we have four "trinities" or groups of three signs, as follows:—

♈ ♉ ♊ | ♋ ♌ ♍ | ♎ ♏ ♐ | ♑ ♒ ♓

each division having a special value and nomenclature of

---

* A concise tabulation of the influence of each separate degree of the zodiac will be found in *Astrology for All, Part I.* p. 241.

its own, in the following order: The first division—Aries, Taurus, and Gemini—is the *intellectual* group; the second division—Cancer, Leo, and Virgo—the *maternal* group; the third division—Libra, Scorpio, and Sagittarius—the *reproductive* group; and, finally—Capricorn, Aquarius, and Pisces —the *serving* group.

It will be seen that these are important divisions, and afford a key to the nature of the angles or cardinal points corresponding to spring, summer, autumn, and winter; spring indicating the intellectual, or budding forth of the green leaves and preparation for the fulness and fruit of summer, the period of energy, youth, and enterprise. It is that period in which we prepare to realize and understand that which is before us.

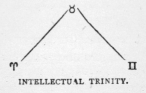

INTELLECTUAL TRINITY.

Of the intellectual group, ♈ ♉ ♊, the first governs the head, as we have seen; it is the pioneer, and thus it ranks first in the external world.

The next sign, ♉, is the focus of this intellectual group. It is the central point or reservoir of the other two, the storehouse in which is reserved the whole of manifested experience; it is the sign of the Sacred Bull. This is the *real* head of the individual, as expressed in the varying modulations of *voice*, and being in direct communication with the heart, for which it is its only true mission to work, it serves as the sheath of the manifesting SOUL. In this sign, then, we have "feeling" and "thinking" striving to become one.

The third, ♊, is, like the first, the external expression of intellect; yet it is strangely dual in its nature, having the mission to express the blending of the soul and the senses, which it strives to do through what is called education, science, and learning; and this sign therefore strongly predisposes to literature, which appeals to both mind and feeling. This group in itself implies the purely intellectual, being the heads of the fiery, earthy, and airy signs, combining spiritual, physical, and mental, and entirely free from the watery or psychic.

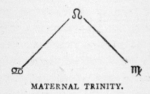

MATERNAL TRINITY.

The next group, ♋ ♌ ♍, is the maternal or maturing principle : under its guidance all the hidden stores of nature are brought forth and ripened into fruit. In it is contained the great trinity of Mother, Father, Son; and of water, fire, and earth; it is the *centre*. Externally it is the metals, and the primary "root" of all that is to be, being governed by the three great factors, Sun, Moon, and Mercury.

The head of the maternal group is the sign ♋, and this moist sign of lunar nature fructifies and germinates the seeds of emotion and the maternal principles. It yields to the influence of external forces. Its work is the preparation of the soil for the rays of the glorious Sun, and by refreshing showers, and the early dews of emotion, it opens up toward the path of devotion. By position, being the fourth of the signs, it is the external expression of all that constitutes maternal feeling in its higher forms.

The central part of the group, ♌, is the nucleus around which all feeling gathers. It is the home and fountain-head of the love element, and from it springs all the life-giving energy of the universe. All feeling and sympathy are refined in this sign, and from it emanates the pure maternal love. It is the nourisher and sustainer: warmth, life, light, and love are matured in this sign. This group is headed by the first of the emotional signs, ♋; but in this sign, ♌, emotion becomes devotion, being purified by transmutation in the baptism of the Solar Fire.

Virgo, ♍, the feet of the maternal group, is also the external expression for the other two, and finds its complete outlet in the physical organism. The vital forces in this sign obtain their highest degree of perfection, and, like the terminating sign of the intellectual trinity, it is dual in its expression, and combines the influence of the two preceding signs. In the commercial world abundant opportunities are offered for the full manifestation of this principle.

This group, it will be seen, is entirely distinct from the former; it may be classed as the division of the HEART, while the first is of the HEAD. It is therefore the unity of these two divisions which must finally constitute perfection; the central point of the intellectual group (♉) being pure mind, or *manas*, while the central of the maternal group (♌) represents the heart, or spirit. Of the first, the externals (♈ ♊) are intellectual, and the centre wisdom; of the second, the externals (♋ ♍) are emotional, and the centre love or devotion. And when the emotions are guided by intellect, and the reason joined with devotion, we have perfect harmony.

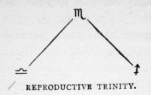

REPRODUCTIVE TRINITY.

The reproductive group, consisting of ♎ ♏ ♐, is again distinctly different from the two former. In this group the combined influence of head and heart is manifested, and this commences what are called the descending signs, signifying the spirit's descent into matter, and its rising to reproduce the original plans matured in the former group. Libra, the point of balance, is the head of the reproductive group, and having combined the influence of ♈ and ♋, or the union of intellect and emotion, it may therefore be considered as the seat of intuition, and being the seventh sign, it gives expression to the whole work of the former six, and by weighing in the "balance" of reason its former experiences it becomes a perfect storehouse of knowledge, and, while resting, is able to reproduce from itself harmony, and finally *intuition*.

The central point of the group, Scorpio, contains the wisdom of the serpent, and this sign gives expression to the combined forces of Taurus and Leo, and therefore becomes the centre of mind and will, which it reproduces in the form of desire. This is the mystical sign, being that portion which is at the foot of the cross, or, in other words, spirit, deeply buried in matter.

A great mystery lies concealed in this sign. Spirit or

life may either expend itself in reproducing through the generative system upon the physical plane, or turn its forces upward again to the spiritual realms, and thus become regenerate. In this sign we have those who are baptized in the waters of emotion, the conquering of which constitutes emancipation from the slavery of sense or desire.

The third sign of this group, Sagittarius, has a mission to reproduce the combined influences of ♊ and ♍, thus transmuting intellect into the wisdom religion, and producing the best divines, or those who are preachers of the Truth. The third and sixth signs are one in this, and in it science and religion must unite and give expression to all that the other three combine. There is much meaning in the symbol of the archer, Sagittarius, who shoots from the bow of image-making power.

In judging the combined influence of the reproductive group, we find each sign reproduces in the world of matter the thoughts and ideas of the intellectual and maternal groups, intellect and emotion (♈ ♋) becoming intuition (♎), and science and poetry (♊ ♍) becoming religion (♐); while the central point contains the essence of *power*, which may either reproduce in forms or soar aloft into the occult or regenerate condition, and, like the phœnix, rise from its ashes into immortality.

The serving trinity comprises Capricorn, Aquarius, and Pisces, the three last signs of the zodiac, and the last extremities of the cardinal, fixed, and common crosses. In the physical world, Capricorn expresses itself best in the politician who single-mindedly serves humanity with intellect. It is the sign of service in its highest external aspect, and constitutes the highest form of honourable service.

SERVING TRINITY.

The internal sign of this group, Aquarius, is the man regenerate; he is now able to serve and aid on humanity to its final goal—Perfection—wherein it may be ready to realize to the full its spiritual power. Herein love and wisdom are blended, and the full attainment of self-consciousness made possible. The ideal manhood may now become a reality so far as the metaphysical world is concerned, for it is the external expression of Leo, and the unfoldment of all that lay concealed in that sign. It is the promise of all that shall be in the seventh race. At present it serves humanity in the supply of metaphysical thought.

Finally, the last sign, Pisces, is the servant upon the lowest rung. This condition may be called the critical state; its action, however, is upon the external plane, and so we have mediums and all those of exceedingly receptive nature coming under the rule of this sign. Its influence corresponds to the great region of the "astral plane," the time for the unfoldment of which has not yet arrived.

It will be clear from the foregoing remarks that the division into these four groups is most important. If we take the heads of each, we shall have the four *Cardinal* signs ♈ ♋ ♎ ♑, which we may class under the heading of the MENTAL group; then the centres ♉ ♌ ♏ ♒, the primary, *Fixed*, or VITAL group; and lastly, the common signs ♊ ♍ ♐ ♓, which we may term the *Mutable,* MOTIVE, or critical groups.

The above, however, is only a brief digest of each division that has been given, and we shall have more to say about the signs when dealing with the True Nature of the Planets. At present the following diagram will convey some idea of the nature of the divisions:—

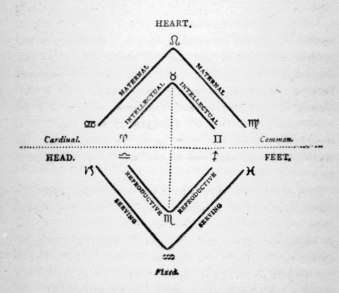

CHAPTER IX

THE TWELVE HOUSES OF THE HEAVENS

WE have hitherto dealt with the signs of the zodiac. We now come to the twelve divisions which are called "houses" or "mansions," as distinct from the signs.

These "houses" are divisions of the heavens which have relation to the *diurnal rotation of the earth on its axis*, as distinguished from its *annual revolution round the Sun*; and the one method of division is analogous to the other in precisely the same way that dawn, noon, sunset, and midnight are respectively analogous to spring, summer, autumn, and winter. Thus the first "house" is analogous to the first "sign," Aries, and is related to the head and to the intellectual activities in general, as expressed in the pioneering and enterprising spirit; and so on with the others, as will be explained later. The use of the word house in such a phrase as "Mars in Capricorn is in the house of its exaltation" should not be confused with the meaning just given, of course. The signs are called the "houses" of the planets, in this sense, it is true, but that has nothing to do with the meaning we are now about to attach to the word. The twelve "(mundane) houses" are constituted by a twelve-fold division of the visible heavens as seen from the birth place at the moment of birth; they differ altogether from the signs, for only under very rare conditions can they completely coincide with them (though they do so more or less approximately *once* during each day). However, all this will be made quite clear as we proceed.

We will now consider the fundamental principles upon

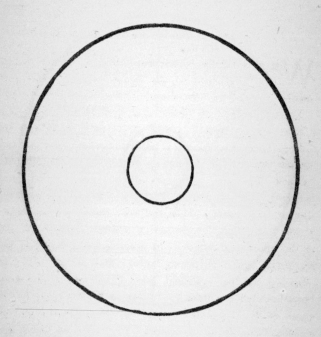

which this twelve-fold division is based. First let us draw two circles as above :—

The inner circle will then represent the Earth, and the outer the visible sphere of the heavens.

Now draw four lines cutting the whole into four equal parts or "quadrants," as shown in the diagram on this page.

These four lines are termed the "angles." That marked E will represent "eastern angle" or Ascendant,* and the

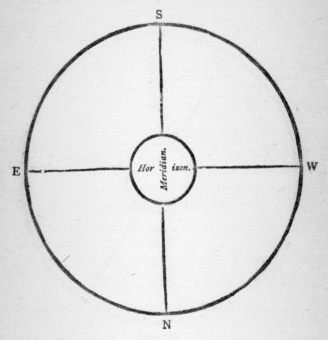

line marked W the western angle or Descendant. The

* Often spoken of as the "Rising Sign." It will be noted that the observer is supposed to be facing South and looking upwards; the point S will therefore be that through which the upper meridian passes, where each planet in turn will culminate, while N indicates that at which they reach their lowest point and again commence their upward path. E and W are the eastern and western points of the horizon where the planets "rise" and "set" respectively.

top of the map marked S will be the midheaven or south point,* and that marked **N** the nadir or north point. These four cardinal points are the most important divisions of the circle, each having a similar "correspondence" in

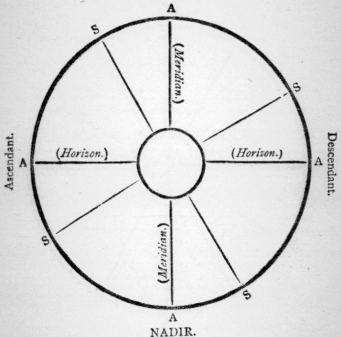

MIDHEAVEN.

NADIR.

the four seasons, Spring, Autumn, Winter, and Summer respectively.

Now let us draw four more lines, one-third of the way between, and call them "succedent" houses, as above.

We have now eight divisions, each line marked **A**

* Where the Sun "souths" at noon.

marking off the "cusp," as it is called, of the four "cardinal" or "angular" houses or "angles"; while the lines marked S, one-third of a right angle (30°) farther on, show at once the extent of these cardinal houses, and mark the "cusps" of the "succedent" houses. Now let us add

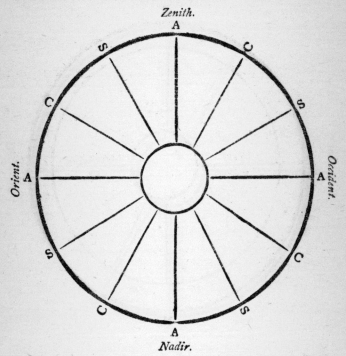

in a similar way four more lines, and call them "cadent" houses, and mark each C for distinction. Then we shall have a circle with twelve equal divisions, as here shown.

As has been said before, the "angles" correspond to the *Cardinal* signs; and similarly the "succedent" houses correspond to the *Fixed*, and the "cadent" to the *Mutable* signs.

We thus have twelve vacant spaces or "houses"; and upon these twelve houses we must now fix our attention, for each has a special and peculiar value of its own, quite distinct and apart from that of any of the others. The

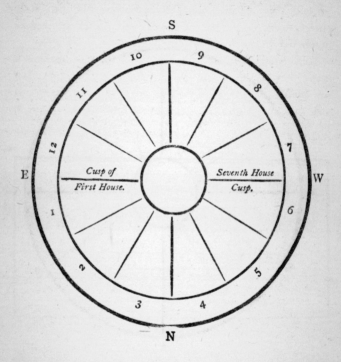

First house we must henceforth know as the ASCENDANT; the *Second house* will be the next to the Ascendant, *i.e.* the first "succedent" house; and the *Third house* will follow, this being the first "cadent" house. The NADIR is always known as the *Fourth house*. Next to it the *fifth*, then the *sixth*, until we come to the DESCENDANT, as we shall in future call the *Seventh house.* Next the eighth, then the ninth, until we come to the M.C., or MIDHEAVEN, which is the *Tenth house.* Then follows the eleventh, and finally the twelfth. To make this clear we will draw another map, this time one with two outer circles, and inside we will place the lines or houses numbered in order. (See opposite page.)

Some students prefer the Indian method of making a map—that is, the square—which is drawn as follows; but we advise the use of the circle maps, for the present at any rate, since the square map is very confusing for a beginner :—

M.C.

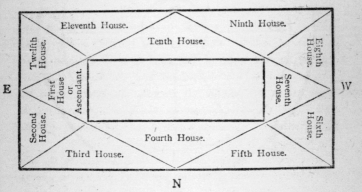

In the circle map it will be seen that each line marks off divisions which are purely "imaginary," but which are needed to distinguish each house from the other. They are called the "cusps" of the houses. The *cusp* of a house is the line between that house and the preceding house, and it represents the line of strongest influence of that house (thus the cusp of the Ascendant, or first

house, is the *horizon*, and the Sun has the greatest power
in that house at the moment of dawn). This is clearly
shown in the diagram.

Each house, we have remarked, has a special value of
its own, and a correct knowledge of the qualities of each
one of the Houses is very important ; but it must always
be considered *secondary* in every way to the influence of
the Signs, which may be termed the fixed or natural
houses, and which have a distinct and permanent meaning.
Probably the best method of distinction would be to call
the twelve signs the fixed or Major Circle, and the twelve
houses or divisions of the heavens the shifting or Minor
Circle. We will now deal with the twelve Houses, referring
again to the difference later on.

The *First House* is what is called the Ascendant, and
governs all matters connected with the life of the person
for whom the map is erected ; from it we also get a
general view of the disposition and condition, and to a
great extent the health. It governs the HEAD. It is the
first angle, the most important, and may be considered as
that portion of the map which chiefly limits and controls
the *personality*, corresponding to sunrise or *dawn*.

The division marked *Second House* has much to do with
the finance or wealth, and the pecuniary position in general
is usually judged from it. It is said to have much to do
with the inner thoughts, which is probable. It governs
the THROAT.

The *Third House* is the portion indicating the intellect
and condition of the mind ; also all matters connected
with brethren, short journeys, letters and papers. Neighbours and the activities are herein denoted. It governs
the LUNGS and NERVES, ARMS and SHOULDERS.

The *Fourth House* presides over the house we live in, the mother, and the end of things. It is sometimes called the grave, which means that it is concerned with all hidden things, such as our private affairs and the ultimate of our present existence: it corresponds to *midnight*. It governs the CHEST, BREASTS, STOMACH, and LIVER.

The *Fifth House* is the portion connected with children and speculation, also cooking and bathing, and all our material and physical pleasures. It has also much to do with our previous life in the physical world. It governs the HEART and BACK.

The *Sixth House* is the portion signifying servants and sickness. It is also the house of phenomenal magic and superstition; also matters likely to bring worry and petty annoyance. It governs the BOWELS and the SOLAR PLEXUS.

The foregoing six Houses are below the earth, and have therefore chiefly to do with the Personality, the "form" side of the nature—the "*mould*," as it were, into which the glowing metal of life is poured.

The *Seventh House* corresponds to sunset, the point where night and day meet and merge into one. It is the house of marriage or union, law and partnership. It governs the REINS and KIDNEYS and the VITAL FLUIDS. It is the house of the Individuality, the "life" side of the nature.

The *Eighth House* is the portion given to "death," or change of existence from one plane of activity to another; and it is hence also connected with wills and legacies. It is the house of occultism, freemasonry, &c. It governs the SECRET PARTS.

The *Ninth House* denotes all matters connected with science, true religion, and the higher learning; also with

E

long journeys, sea voyages, &c. It is the house of "new birth." It governs the THIGHS, and to some extent the NERVES.

The *Tenth House*, or midheaven, is concerned with honour, the employment or profession, employers, the moral qualities, and the fathers: it corresponds to *noon*. It governs the KNEES.

The *Eleventh House* is given to friends, hopes, desires, and wishes; acquaintances and associates. It governs the ANKLES and the BLOOD.

The *Twelfth House* has to do with all private matters, such as secret enemies, imprisonment, persecution, worry, sorrow, and misery. It is the house of deep occultism. It governs the FEET.

These last six Houses are those that are above the earth; and they relate to the higher or divine side of man's nature—the living "*metal*," to revert to our former simile.

There have been various opinions expressed about these twelve divisions, some doubting whether they have any important influence in nativities, and contending that their only value is in connection with Horary Astrology. Experience alone can be the true teacher; but we have tested the matter, and find they have sufficient importance to include them in this work. Nevertheless our remarks following the map of the twelve houses should not be forgotten; for this is in reality the Minor Circle, and its overcoming is the first attempt to escape LIMITATION. That is to say, when the influence of the various planets in their respective *houses* begins to wane, the planets manifesting their nature through the various *signs*, the soul may be said to be taking its first steps upon the "path of liberation."

CHAPTER X

HOW TO CAST THE HOROSCOPE

WE have now come to the stage where it is necessary to learn how to cast the horoscope. This we consider the most simple proceeding of all. It is said that any one can cast the nativity, even a child, but few can judge it when it is cast; and this is true. With a little practice the erecting of the map becomes a very easy matter; all that is necessary is an ephemeris for the year required, and a "Table of Houses" for the place of birth: the publishers of this book will supply the former for any year. The method to be explained is very simple, but it is not therefore inexact.*

For the purposes of illustration let us take "Raphael's" *Ephemeris* for the year 1896. If it is opened at the month of June, say, it will be noticed that the longitude,†

---

* ACCURACY *versus* PRECISION.—It is necessary to distinguish in thought between "accuracy" and "precision." *Precision* implies extreme definition in detail; which may be compared to a sharply focused photograph. *Accuracy* merely demands that the map should be correct within the margin of error implied in the figuring; which may be compared to a drawing, correct as to shading and perspective. Thus, the map shown on page 81 would be *accurate* if it gave the Ascendant as ♏ 20°, ♅ ♏ 22°, ☉ ♊ 13°, &c.; though not *precise*. On the other hand, if the Ascendant were put down as either ♏ 21° or ♏ 20° 0' and ♅ as ♏ 21° or 22° 0', &c., it would be not only lacking in "precision," but also inaccurate, because misleading. Ordinary carefulness and plain common-sense are far more useful to the student of Astrology than great ability in figuring.

† The longitude of a planet is its zodiacal position.

67

latitude, and declination of the planets are given in various columns. A copy of part of pages 12 and 13 we give as follows :—

12   JUNE, 1896.   [RAPHAEL'S

D.	Neptune.		Herschel.		Saturn.		Jupiter.		Mars.			
M.	Lat.	Dec.	Lat.	Dec.	Lat.	Dec.	Lat.	Dec.	Lat.	Dec.		
	° ′	° ′	° ′	° ′	° ′	° ′	° ′	° ′	° ′	° ′	° ′	
1	1 S 22	21 N 30	0 N 17	17 S 55	2 N 31	13 S 38	0 N 41	19 N 34	1 S 41	1 N 39	1 N 56
3	1 22	21 30	0 17	17 54	2 31	13 36	0 41	19 29	1 41	2 13	

								MIDNIGHT.	
D. M.	D. W.	Sidereal Time.	☉ Long.	☉ Dec.	☽ Long.	☽ Lat.	☽ Dec.	☽ Long.	☽ Dec.
		H. M. S.	° ′ ″	° ′	° ′ ″	° ′	° ′	° ′ ″	° ′
1	M.	4 41 52	11 ♋ 25 34	22 N 10	20 ♒ 58 41	0 S 36	15 S 5	27 ♒ 6 29	12 S 32
2	Tu.	4 45 49	12 23 1	22 18	3 ♓ 10 25	0 N 29	9 54	9 ♓ 11 8	7 12
3	W.	4 49 45	13 20 26	22 25	15 ♓ 9 17	1 31	4 27	21 ♓ 5 34	1 41

On page 12 it will be seen that latitude and declination only of the planets in top columns are given. The *latitude* of the planet means the distance it is North or South of the ecliptic; its value will be seen later: for the present it may be ignored. The *declination* means the distance of the planet North or South of the equator; it will be remembered that when speaking of aspects the par. dec. (same distance North or South of equator) was said to be equivalent to a conjunction (☌).

In the columns marked off below the latitude and

declination of planets, a column marked *Sidereal Time* will be seen. It is from this sidereal time that we discover the rising sign, for it represents the position

D.	Venus.			Mercury.			☽ Node.	Mutual Aspects.
M.	Lat.	Declination.		Lat.	Declination.			
	° ′	° ′	° ′	° ′	° ′	° ′	° ′	(1) ♀ P ♃
1	0 S 44	19 N 41	19 N 58	0 S 44	22 N 34	22 N 16	28 ♒ 27	(2) ☉ P ☿
3	0 39	20 14	20 30	1 20	21 58	21 40	28 30	(3) ☉ 150 ♄
5	0 34	20 46		1 54	21 21		28 14	(5) ♀ ✳ ♃
								☿ Q ♂, P ♅

D.	♅ Long.	♆ Long.	♄ Long.	♃ Long.	♂ Long.	♀ Long.	☿ Long.	Lunar Aspects.						
M.								☉	☿	♅	♄	♃	♂	♀	☿
	° ′	° ′	° ′	° ′	° ′	° ′	° ′							
1	17 ♊ 32	21 ♍ 42	13 ♏ 57	5 ♌ 36	8 ♈ 4	1 ♊ 4	24 ♊ 10	△	□				∠		△
2	17 34	21 ℞ 40	13 ℞ 53	5 46	8 48	2 17	23 ℞ 54						⩝		□
3	17 37	21 37	13 50	5 56	9 32	3 30	23 34	□	□		△	⊡			

of the meridian (M.C.) *at noon* each day. If we want to know the value of the meridian before noon, we must deduct from this sidereal time the number of hours between the time required and noon; if after noon, then we must add. This gives us the *Sidereal time at birth*, often called the R.A.M.C. What these letters mean it is unnecessary to explain here, as the astronomical details concerned with horoscopes will be fully treated of in a later work.* There is what is called a *Table of Houses*

* *Astrology for All*, Part II., price 7s. 6d.

given at the end of " Raphael's " *Ephemeris*, and owing to this arrangement the whole work of erecting the map is simplified. Below we give a part copy of these tables of houses for the latitude of London : tables of houses for other latitudes may be procured.

TABLE OF HOUSES FOR LONDON, LAT. 51° 32′ N.

Sidereal Time.	10 ♈	11 ♉	12 ♊	Asc. ♋		2 ♌	3 ♍	Sidereal Time.	10 ♊	11 ♋	12 ♌	Asc. ♍		2 ♍	3 ♎
H. M. S.	°	°	°	°	′	°	°	H. M. S.	°	°	°	°	′	°	°
0 0 0	0	9	22	26	36	12	3	3 51 15	0	8	11	7	21	28	25
0 18 21	5	14	26	29	55	16	7	4 12 13	5	12	15	11	2	♎ 2	♏
0 44 8	12	21	♋ 2	4 ♌ 33		21	13	4 41 59	12	19	21	16	15	8	7
0 47 50	13	22	3	5	12	22	14	4 46 16	13	20	21	17	0	9	8
1 47 48	29	♊ 8	16	15	48	♍ 4	27	5 55 38	29	♌ 5	♍ 5	29	13	23	23

We have chosen the first and third columns of page 26, also the first, sixth, thirteenth, fourteenth, and thirtieth lines for explanation.

Now we will suppose we wish to erect a map for noon on 2nd June 1896, London. Our first proceeding would be to find the sidereal time for that moment, and as the map was for London, we should then refer to the table of houses for that latitude and find its equivalent in sidereal time. On 2nd June 1896, the sidereal time at noon is 4 h. 45 min. 49 sec. ; and on looking at the table of houses

we find 4 h. 46 min. 16 sec., the figures nearest to these.
If we place a piece of note-paper just under this
4 h. 46 min. 16 sec. we shall have in view a line of figures
as follows :—

| 4   46   16 | 13 | 20 | 21 | 17   0 | 9 | 8 |

A piece of blank paper.

On referring to the head of the column we shall find the
signs of the zodiac as follows :—

10	11	12	Ascen.	2	3
♊	♋	♌	♍	♍	♎

This means that those signs are on the houses as
numbered : 10 means the tenth house or M.C., 11 the
eleventh house, 12 the twelfth ; *Ascen.* the Ascendant,
2 the second house, and 3 the third. However, if we
were to place these signs upon our six houses we should
be in error ; for as we come down each column of figures
we find some different signs are placed in that line where
there would have been figures, indicating that that sign
has now passed the "cusp" of that house, and that a new
sign has arrived thereat. Let us, then, fix up our houses
with their signs allotted to each. Our marker gave us a
line of figures which indicated the number of degrees upon
each house, and as we found the value of each house at
the head of each line, we will mark them down in a row
as follows : 10, 11, 12, Ascen., 2, 3.

Now we must find the signs on each house, which are
as follows : ♊ ♋ ♌ ♍ ♎ ♏. Now the degrees thus :
13°, 20°, 21°, 17° 0′, 9°, 8°. Now if we place these in

lines, in the above order, we may prepare a scale as follows :—

10th.	11th.	12th.	Ascen.	2nd.	3rd.	*Houses.*
♊	♋	♌	♍	♎	♏	*Signs*
13°	20°	21°	17° 0′	9°	8°	*Degrees*

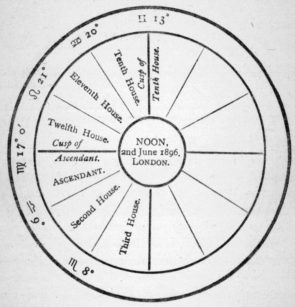

Now all is ready to fill into the map. Place ♊ 13° on the tenth house or midheaven; ♋ 20° on the eleventh house, ♌ 21° on the twelfth, and ♍ 17° 0′ on the Ascendant; ♎ 9° on the second, and ♏ 8° on the third, and our map will look as shown above.

It will be at once seen that only six of the houses have been filled in, so that we are six short. Now, we remember that the signs that fall on opposite houses are the signs that are opposite each other; we therefore fill them in, as follows : ♐ is opposite to ♊, so place ♐ 13° on the fourth house, ♑ is opposite to ♋, so ♑ 20° comes on the fifth, ♒ 21° on the sixth, ♓ 17° on the seventh, ♈ 9° on the eighth, and ♉ 8° on the ninth, and our map stands as follows :—

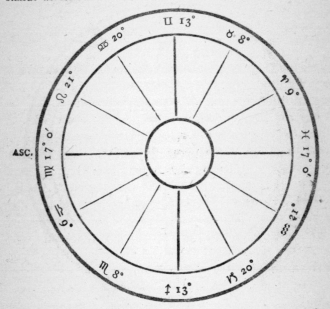

Now, let us venture a little farther and erect a map for 1.24 P.M., 2nd June 1896. As before, we find the sidereal time at noon is 4 h. 45 min. 49 sec., so we must *add* 1 h. 24 min. to this, it being *after* noon, thus :—

$$
\begin{array}{rrr}
4 & 45 & 49 \\
1 & 24 & 0 \\
\hline
6 & 9 & 49 \\
\end{array}
$$

This total, 6 h. 9 min. 49 sec., will be the sidereal time for

1.24 P.M., and to know the signs and houses for this we
must again refer to the table of houses to find the nearest
figures to 6 h. 9 min. 49 sec. This we find near the top of
the lower left-hand column, page 26 in the *Ephemeris*,
which gives us the houses, &c., as follows :—

10th.	11th.	12th.	Ascen.	2nd.	3rd.	Houses.
♋	♌	♍	♎	♎	♏	Signs
2°	8°	8°	1° 33′	26°	26°	Degrees

But now we have something different. If these figures
and signs be fitted to their respective houses it will be
found that one sign, ♎, occupies *two* houses, *i.e.* the
Ascendant and the second house. This causes what is
called an "intercepted" sign, and this intercepted sign
must be placed in the house between the signs where it
is missing. The missing sign is here Sagittarius (♐), and
it must be placed in the third house, between ♏, which
falls on the cusp of the third house, and ♑, which being
opposite to ♋ falls upon the cusp of the fourth house.
Care must be taken always to fill in the opposite sign
to the one intercepted, as well as the latter; in this case
it is ♊, placed in the ninth house.

Now let us erect a map for *before* noon—say, 9.2 A.M.,
same day. Again we refer to sidereal time for noon, 2nd
June, and from this 4 h. 45 min. 49 sec. we deduct
2 h. 58 min. as follows :—

$$
\begin{array}{rrr}
4 & 45 & 49 \\
2 & 58 & 0 \\
\hline
1 & 47 & 49 \\
\end{array}
$$

this 2 h. 58 min. is the difference between 9.2 A.M. and
noon. Then we refer to the table of houses for London

again, and we find sidereal time 1 h. 47 min. 49 sec. at
the foot of the first column, and this gives us :—

10th.	11th.	12th.	Ascen.	2nd.	3rd.	Houses.
♈	♊	♋	♌	♍	♍	Signs
29°	8°	16°	15° 48′	4°	27°	Degrees

Again an intercepted sign, this time ♉ in the tenth house
or midheaven.

The foregoing will give the beginner some idea of how
to cast the figure, and in all cases where the birth time is
not known with absolute accuracy, it will be quite exact
enough if the birth place is anywhere near London or
the South of England.   To be quite accurate, however,
we must proceed in the following manner :—

Required a map of the heavens for 7 P.M., 5th June
1896, London.

	H.	M.	S.
Sidereal time, noon, 5th June 1896, London .	4	57	38
For seven hours, P.M., *plus* . . .	7	0	0
Correction of mean to sidereal time, *plus* .	0	1	10
Sidereal time for 7 P.M., 5th June, London .	11	58	48

The equivalent of this is ♍ 29° 40′, which must be placed
in the M.C., and from this the degrees on the cusp of the
others are obtained in the usual way, by simple proportion.
Thus, at 11 h. 56 min. 20 sec. S.T. the Ascen. is ♐ 2° 43′, at
12 h. 0 min. 0 sec. it is ♐ 3° 23′—*diff*. 40′ for 3 min. 40 sec. ;
therefore *diff*. for 1 min. 13 sec. = 13′; so put ♐ 3° 23′
minus 13′, *i.e.* ♐ 3° 10′, on the Ascendant.   Thus always for
the Midheaven and Ascendant, but the nearest degree will do
for the other houses.

The correction from mean to sidereal time should always be used; if *after* noon, add; if *before* noon, deduct. The following is the table of corrections:—

Mean Time.	Correction.	Mean Time.	Correction.	Mean Time.	Correction.
Hours.	Min. Sec.	Hours.	Min. Sec.	Min.	Sec.
1	0 9.86	7	1 9.00	5	0.82
2	0 19.71	8	1 18.85	10	1.64
3	0 29.57	9	1 28.71	15	2.46
4	0 39.43	10	1 38.57	30	4.93
5	0 49.28	11	1 48.42	45	7.39
6	0 59.14	12	1 58.28		

FOREIGN HOROSCOPES.

When horoscopes are required for births occurring abroad, or indeed for any place out of London, the true local mean time must be ascertained, as well as the Greenwich time, and the houses of the horoscope calculated for the former, while the planets are calculated for the latter.

But all such details are explained, more fully than space permits here, in the work before alluded to, *Astrology for All, Part II*. For the present it will be enough to say that the GOLDEN RULE in casting horoscopes is: Calculate the houses for *True Local Mean Time*, and the planets for *Greenwich Mean Time* (G.M.T.).

The difference between local and Greenwich time in England, it may be remarked, never exceeds a quarter of an hour, and therefore it is hardly necessary to take account of it except where the birth-time is known with tolerable exactitude. But for the sake of clearness an example may be given.

True local time at any place depends upon the longitude of the place East or West of Greenwich : for places E. of Greenwich it is, at any given moment, *more* than the Greenwich time, and for places W. of Greenwich *less* ; each degree of longitude being equivalent to four minutes of time.

EXAMPLE.—*Required, a map for* 6 P.M. (*Greenwich time*), *2nd June* 1896, *at Liverpool : longitude* 2° 59′ W.

	H.	M.	S.
Sidereal time, noon, 2nd June 1896, G.M.T., at London	4	45	49
For six hours, P.M. (*plus*)	6	0	0
Correction of mean to sidereal time	0	1	0
Sid. time for 6 P.M., 2nd June 1896, G.M.T., at London	10	46	49
Time equivalent to 2° 59′ W. at 4 min. per degree (*minus*)	0	11	56
Sidereal time for 6 P.M., 2nd June 1896, AT LIVERPOOL	10	34	53

It will be seen on comparing this result with the sidereal time or R.A.M.C. for the same moment *at London*, which will be needed for our next example, that there is a considerable difference, as regards the HOUSES, between two horoscopes cast for *the same moment of time* respectively for London and Liverpool, though the planetary positions would of course be identical in both cases.

Different Tables of Houses are required according to the latitude of the birth place : tables for Liverpool and New York are given in "Raphael's" *Ephemeris.*

CHAPTER XI

HOW TO PLACE THE PLANETS IN THE MAP

HAVING erected the map, we now proceed to fill in the planets. The longitudes of the planets given in the *Ephemeris* for 2nd June 1896, at noon, are as follows :—

⊙ Ⅱ 12°23′, ☽ ♓ 3°10′, ☿ Ⅱ 23°54′ ℞, ♀ Ⅱ 2°17′, ♂ ♈ 8°48′, ♃ ♌ 5°46′, ♄ ♏ 13°53′ ℞, ♅ ♏ 21°40′ ℞, ♆ Ⅱ 17°34′.

Now if a map is required for P.M. or after noon of that day, the places of the planets on the *following* day must be noted, in order to get at their rates of motion : to enable the student to check the calculations, we give the motion of each planet during the day of twenty-four hours between the second and third of June, ⊙ 57′ 25″; ☽ 12°; ☿ 20′ (decreasing); ♀ 1° 13′; ♂ 44′; ♃ 10′; ♄ 3′ (decreasing); ♅ 3′ (decreasing); ♆ 3′.

At the end of "Raphael's" *Ephemeris* there is a table of proportional logarithms, with an explanation of their use, which the beginner will do well to study, since it is perfectly simple and saves a great deal of time and labour. To those, however, who prefer to work in the old way, the above motion of the planets must be divided by twenty-four to get the motion per hour, and this multiplied by the number of hours before or after noon; the result being added or subtracted, as the case may be, to or from the position at noon. In this way the planets' positions at the time of birth must be severally found, and the same duly inserted in the map. The Sun moves about $2\frac{1}{2}$ minutes per hour, but the other planets vary, so the proportion must always be obtained from the daily motion. In many cases it is sufficient to find the ☽'s place, and insert the other planets as if for noon.

If we were erecting a map for noon, we should fill in the planets' places into the map given in the last chapter, as they are in the *Ephemeris*. We should then have the Sun on the midheaven in ♊ 12° 23′; the Moon would be in the sixth house in ♓ 3° 10′; ☿ in the tenth in ♊ 23° 54′ ℞; ♀ in the ninth in ♊ 2° 17′; ♂ just entering the eighth, in ♈ 8° 48′; ♃ in the eleventh in ♌ 5° 46′; ♄ in the third in ♏ 13° 53′ ℞; ♅ in the third in ♏ 21° 40′ ℞; ♆ in the tenth in ♊ 17° 34′.

Let us erect a map for 6 P.M., 2nd June 1896, London.

	H.	M.	S.
The sidereal time at noon, 2nd June, G.M.T., is	4	45	49
Add for 6 P.M.	6	0	0
Correction for six hours	0	0	59.14
Sidereal time for 6 P.M. . . .	10	46	48.14

Having obtained this sidereal time, we look in the table of houses at the end of "Raphael's" *Ephemeris*, and find the nearest to this is 10 *h.* 46 *m.* 9 *s.*, for which we have the following :—

10	11	12	Ascen.	2	3
♍ 10°	♎ 11°	♏ 3°	20° ♏ 11′	♐ 21°	♒ 0°

The opposite signs are :—

4	5	6	7	8	9
♓ 10°	♈ 11°	♉ 3°	20° ♉ 11′	♊ 21°	♌ 0°

The intercepted signs are :—

♑ in the second, and ♋ in the eighth.

The planets' places and their respective daily motions must now be noted, and these we have given above.

We will next proceed to find their positions at 6 P.M. Four times six are twenty-four, therefore we shall require to divide the daily motion by four to find their true positions. Taking the Sun, whose motion is 57′ 25″, by dividing by four, we find its motion for the six hours will be 14′ 21″.

	°	′	″
Thus we add to the place at noon . . . ♊	12	23	1
	0	14	21
Total : Sun's place for 6 P.M. . . . . ♊	12	37	22

Taking the Moon next, whose motion we find is 12°, this is 30′ per hour, or 1 degree per two hours. If we divide 12° by four we shall find that in six hours the Moon will have moved 3 degrees; this added to the Moon's place at noon, ♓ 3° 10′ 25″, gives us ♓ 6° 10′ 25″. Mercury is decreasing 20′ in the twenty-four hours; that is going backward, or what is called retrograde. A fourth of 20′ being 5′, this must be deducted from its place at noon. Thus 23° 54′, less 5′, is 23° 49′; and so on with the other planets; and we have them calculated for 6 P.M. as follows : *—

☉ 12° 37′ 22″ ♊	♀ 2° 35′ ♊	♂ 8° 59′ ♈
☽ 6° 10′ 25″ ♓	♃ 5° 48′ ℞ ♌	♄ 13° 52′ ℞ ♏
☿ 23° 49′ ♊ ℞	♅ 21° 39′ ♏ ℞	♆ 17° 35′ ♊

* The symbol ℞ signifies *retrograde*, and is used to show that the apparent motion of the planet, as viewed from the earth, is in the direction ♈ ♓ ♒ . . . instead of ♈ ♉ ♊ . . . as is ordinarily the case. The astronomical reasons for this phenomenon need not be entered upon here. All the planets are ℞ at certain times, but ☉ and ☽ never are.

The map will now be as follows:—

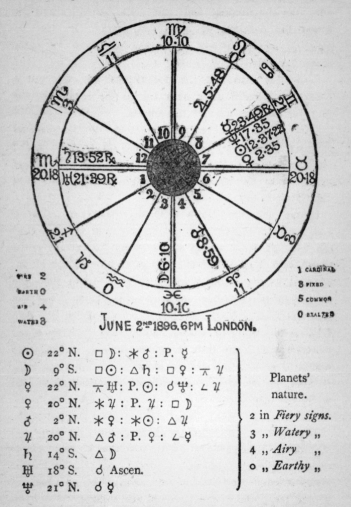

JUNE 2ND 1896. 6PM LONDON.

☉	22° N.	□ ☽ : ✱ ♂ : P. ☿
☽	9° S.	□ ☉ : △ ♄ : □ ♀ : ⊼ ♃
☿	22° N.	⊼ ♅ : P. ☉ : ♂ ♅ : ∠ ♃
♀	20° N.	✱ ♃ : P. ♃ : □ ☽
♂	2° N.	✱ ♀ : ✱ ☉ : △ ♃
♃	20° N.	△ ♂ : P. ♀ : ∠ ☿
♄	14° S.	△ ☽
♅	18° S.	♂ Ascen.
♆	21° N.	♂ ☿

Planets'
nature.

2 in *Fiery signs.*
3 „ *Watery* „
4 „ *Airy* „
0 „ *Earthy* „

Now the declinations of the planets are obtained in the

F

same way, and proportioned exactly as we have done
with the longitudes, and can thus be calculated to
obtain the positions as given (*see map*). (It must be
borne in mind, however, that some are given for every
second day only.)

From this map and the declinations we work out a
"speculum," which gives us a key to the reading of the
map, for in it we tabulate the aspects.

These aspects are reckoned as taught in the previous
chapters. The *Fiery* signs are each in trine to each;
similarly also the *Earthy*, *Airy*, and *Watery*. The *Fixed*
signs are in mutual square or opposition; similarly also
the *Cardinal* and *Mutable*.

In our map the Moon is in the watery sign Pisces,
and "applies" to the Sun in the airy sign Gemini; thus
the Sun and Moon are in square aspect. It will be noted
that Saturn is in 13° of ♏; this is in trine to the Moon.
Mars is in the cardinal and fiery sign Aries, while the
Sun is in the common and airy sign Gemini; thus the
Sun is sextile to Mars, but Jupiter, who is in the fiery sign
Leo, is in trine to Mars. Moon and Venus are in
common signs, and thus in square aspect. Venus is in
sextile to Jupiter, and also to Mars.

From the above we can tabulate the aspects as printed
under the map, *q.v.*

With *practice* the whole work of casting the map and
calculating the planets' places becomes a very simple
matter. There are plenty of works now obtainable, the
cheapest and simplest of all being *The Horoscope in
Detail*, the price of which is only one shilling.

It is not in erecting the horoscope, but in the *iudgmen*

of it, that the difficulty lies, and we shall proceed to make this as simple and complete as it is possible for us to do. The method adopted is one never before published, and, as far as we are aware, never yet attempted by any writer on the subject.

CHAPTER XII

THE VARIOUS BRANCHES OF ASTROLOGY

BEFORE entering fully into the mysteries of this wonderful science, we must first clearly understand the nature of the branch which we are studying. Astrology is divided into four main divisions, each requiring a distinct and separate method of judgment.

The *first* has been called Genethliacal or Horoscopical Astrology, being chiefly concerned with the destiny and fate of the individual born at a certain moment for which a map of the heavens has been cast; *second*, that which is called Horary Astrology; *third*, Mundane or National Astrology; and *fourth*, Astro-Meteorology, or the study of the weather.

Unfortunately the first two branches have become well-nigh hopelessly mixed and entangled, so that there are few real and true astrologers at the present day. Few seem to be able to appreciate the wide difference between the birth of a thought and the birth of a human being. The latter has come into physical manifestation with the definite object of gaining the knowledge and experience required to further its evolution, and deals with the result of causes previously set in motion prior to its taking up its present form. For to the Ego the map is a chart on which is plainly marked the various stages of its growth and evolution, from the drawing in of the first breath until its final outbreathing; the extent of its fate and freewill is clearly shown, also the latent powers capable of awakening and further development until attainment of complete self-consciousness is reached.

But with regard to Horary Astrology no such powers exist, and therefore its symbology remains limited to the world of concrete manifestation, its chief concern being with inanimate objects or passing currents of thought that affect the personality only.

The exposition of the branch under consideration—*i.e.* nativities—will occupy the whole of the present volume. Every theory advanced will be practically illustrated by horoscopes that have had our special attention, and some attempt will be made to fix a definite rule whereby the exact working out of each symbol and aspect will explain the workings of the one universal Law. We must not, however, identify the principles with the symbology used, but regard them as lying at the back of the symbols, so to speak, using the latter only to convey a more definite and concise idea of the plan by which our evolution is moving on toward law and order. From experience alone can we gain knowledge, and in accordance with the experience we have had, so shall we be the better able to judge the symbology when presented to us. Then will knowledge give us power, and by this power may we obtain our liberty, for that is the aim of the student of Astrology—*the power to know himself*, his freedom being limited until this goal is attained. Then will he be free to help and assist others by pointing out to them the just working of the law But to benefit humanity thoroughly he must understand himself, and therefore this must be the aim of every student—to learn exactly what our symbology means, and through those symbols to watch the working of the grand principles behind. Each planet is the symbol of a *principle* in Nature, corresponding to every phase of manifestation on the physical globe.

Now, we cannot "alter" these principles; but we *can* use them wisely, and allow the highest vibrations of which the horoscope is capable to manifest. A complete understanding, therefore, of the true nature of each planet will be our first study, this being the most essential knowledge for the astrologer to obtain before judging the planet's influence upon human life. The ordinary text-books gives us the result of the positions and aspects it is true, but none have hitherto sought out the causes *why* those planets and aspects correspond to certain manifestations.

We shall therefore now proceed to explain the true nature of the planets.

CHAPTER XIII

THE TRUE NATURE OF THE VARIOUS PLANETS

EACH planet is the representative of a principle, and we may watch our own progress by the relationship these symbols hold to each other at birth, and the positions in which we find them in the zodiac.

Astrologers have long associated the various qualities that we express with the planets. Through Mercury we express the *mind*: Venus, *love* and *emotion*: Mars, *force* and *energy*: Jupiter, *sympathy*, *devotion*, and the *higher thought*: Saturn, the *solid*, *heavy*, and *laborious* motions of life. Finally, the Sun and Moon serve as the *time markers;* the former corresponding to the small hand serves to mark off the moral qualities and the higher principles, while the Moon as the collector of the planets' rays acts as the prime transmitter of the planetary influence. The Moon represents the *mortal* part of our life, and the Sun the *immortal;* the former all that comprises our "fate" or Personality, the latter all that contains our "destiny" or Individuality.

Taking the planets in the order of the signs of the zodiac, MARS rules the first sign ♈ (Aries), his "day" house, has his exaltation in ♑ (Capricorn), and his fall in ♋ (Cancer); he also rules as his "night" house the eighth sign ♏ (Scorpio), and has his detriment in ♉ (Taurus). Mars has influence, therefore, over three orders

87

—the fiery, earthy, and watery, but has no affinity with the airy signs, having his detriment in Libra, an airy sign. The signs ♌ and ♐ are of his own nature—fiery—and opposite to these are the airy signs ♒ and ♊, uncongenial to his nature; but the weakest sign of all for Mars appears to be Cancer: here he is opposite to his exaltation and in square to his own day house ♈, though in trine to his night house ♏. The signs ♈ ♌ ♐ ♏ ♑ would therefore seem to offer the best opportunities for the expression of Mars, the planet of energy, strength, courage, life-force, and expansion. The houses best suited for him to give the most marked expression would accordingly be the first, fifth, eighth, ninth, and tenth, corresponding to the signs just mentioned.

Next in order would come VENUS, ruling as her night house the second sign ♉ (Taurus), and the seventh sign ♎ (Libra), as her day house. She has her exaltation in ♓ (Pisces), a watery sign. Here we have sympathy with earth, air, and water; but none with fire, for she has her detriment in ♈ (Aries), as also in Scorpio. We may then judge she would find sympathy in ♉ ♊ ♋ ♎ ♓. She is a powerful influence in all love affairs, and also in everything that has in it the elements of refinement. She is the goddess of love and beauty, and her influence is soothing and inspiring. She would find her best houses in the second, third, fourth, seventh, and twelfth.

The planet MERCURY is the next in order, ruling as his day house the third sign ♊ (Gemini), and as his night house the sixth ♍ (Virgo), having exaltation in the latter.*

* Some thinkers consider that a planet cannot have its exaltation in its own house, and they therefore assign ♒ to ☿ as its exaltation.

Air and earth have here chief rule, so that Mercury would be strongest in the signs ♊ ♍ ♎ ♑ ♒, his weakest influence coming from Sagittarius and Pisces. Mercury is a general significator of the mind, and is one of the chief planets to observe in the horoscope. He is decidedly "convertible," as the old authors express it, for, like the mind, he is impressed first with this and then that, taking in all the influences with which it comes in contact. When in the fixed signs he gives more concentration, but in ♈, ♓, or ♋ he gives a fickle mind, always changing from one thing to another. The houses best suited to Mercury are the third, sixth, seventh, tenth, and eleventh. In all matters where the mind is concerned, give to Mercury first consideration.

Next in order comes THE MOON, whose only sign is ♋ (Cancer); her exaltation is in ♉ (Taurus), and her fall in ♏ (Scorpio), while her detriment is in ♑ (Capricorn). She is the collector of aspects and influences, and acts only in accordance with the sign that she is in, having no definite nature of her own; she is in fact coloured, as it were, by the sign through which she passes. Her best houses are the second, third, fourth, sixth, and ninth, and the worst the fifth and eighth. Her office and mission is *to reflect the light*. As she passes out from the Sun she gathers up the influences on her way until she reaches the full ; thence she returns laden with the fruits of experience to the Sun, and once more re-emerges, cleansed for a new experience. Each month we see her issue forth as a rib from the side of the solar orb, waxing stronger each day as she progresses on her journey among the seven planets. She is the "long hand" of the celestial clock, so to speak, marking off the minutes, the Sun himself representing the "short hand," and the month being the hours. The Moon is often treated as the most important planet in the horoscope, but she is only a servant of the Sun, whose work she sets out to accomplish. Her position must always be noted, and her aspects carefully tabulated: when "separating," her influence is always more marked than when "applying." She is more powerful above the earth than below, and stronger in the magnetic quarters of the horoscope—*i.e.* the second, third, fourth, and the seventh, eighth, and ninth houses.

Coming next, THE SUN rules the sign ♌ (Leo), which is his only house. He is exalted in the fiery sign ♈ (Aries). His detriment and fall occur respectively in ♒ (Aquarius) and ♎ (Libra). He is weak in the watery and earthy, but has great power in the three fiery signs. He improves the benefits of each house he may be in. Spring and summer are his periods; therefore Aries, Taurus, Gemini, Cancer, Leo, and Virgo, and their corresponding houses, constitute his best positions. He is the essence of the Individual, and his position indicates the spot from which the energy of the figure comes. The degree he holds at birth is a vital point. Generally he indicates the Will, and all that is lofty and aspiring.

We now pass on to the planet JUPITER, ruler of the signs ♐ (Sagittarius) and ♓ (Pisces): he has his detriment in ♊ and ♍, and his fall in ♑, being exalted in ♋. This is considered the greater fortune, the giver of all blessings, the god who walked among men; he is the planet of joy, hope, unbounded sympathy, and true generosity. His place in human affairs is connected with the religious part of man's nature, and so governs the higher self. His signs are the ninth and twelfth, and his exaltation is the fourth.

Thus he has chief rule over the last of the signs in the zodiac and also the fourth sign, corresponding to the fourth house, which latter is "the end" in the natal figure. He has sympathy also with the second, fifth, seventh, and ninth houses, and he performs a most important part in our higher evolution.

The next planet we shall deal with is SATURN, who rules the tenth and eleventh signs, having his exaltation in the seventh. This is always considered the greater infortune, for he is the planet of *limitation:* where the Sun's influence ends, there Saturn's begins. All things connected with tact, steady thought, and contemplation come under his ruling influence. He is chiefly concerned with that part of us which is most deeply immersed in matter, and at every step in life we must pass his limitations before we can progress. And so he is the planet of sorrow, because pain is the only teacher, and the more we free ourselves from our own self-made limitations, the more nearly do we approach true liberation. We may always expect his most serious aspects to operate upon the lowest mental plane, which finally works out directly upon the physical.

We now come to that most important planet Herschel or URANUS, the "houseless wanderer," the planet of freedom and of liberty. All that is unlimited and unbound comes under the dominant influence of Uranus, the planet of sudden events and original thought. His mission is to awaken and revivify the slumbering soul, and with thunderbolt catastrophes and lightning-like flashes of intelligence he destroys, re-models, and renews the life of those who come under his magic power. Swift and unexpected, he brings experience unthought of; for with

him indeed it is "the unexpected that always happens."
All metaphysical thought and advanced views find in him
a leader; in fact his influence is so marked and romantic,
that once it is felt it never can be forgotten. He waits
to afflict, but out of his evil good always comes. He
gives no warning of the nature of his catastrophes, but
comes laden, as it were, with a mixture of colours, the
hues of which are peculiarly interwoven with the colour of
the planet that he meets; and the result is a strange
agglomeration of misfortunes such as cannot be mistaken
for those due to any other planet. Gradually, as time
passes on, we see that this planet is destined to play the
most important part in our future evolution. When we
occupy as our home the planet Mercury, that planet will
find its successor in Uranus; but then our minds will
have become so refined that we shall feel the finer
vibrations which will pour into us through the Uranian
influence, and the scope of our intellectual vision will have
then so widened as to enable us to accomplish easily what
would now be gigantic feats of inner perception.

What part the planet NEPTUNE is destined to play we
are not called upon here to describe, for there are few
who at present come under his influence. With regard
to this planet, we shall have more to say in a subsequent
treatise.*

It will now be as well to tabulate under separate head-
ings the influence of the planets in the various depart-
ments of life, taking them in the order we have given
them.

It should be noted that the bodily descriptions given are

* See *How to Judge a Nativity, Part II.,* Chapter III.

those of the pure types; such are very rare, being in most cases greatly modified by aspects received from other planets.

MARS.

The nature of Mars is choleric, hot and dry, expansive, bold, impulsive, energetic, courageous, and distinctive. He makes the body strong, the stature of middle height, big boned, but not fat, with round face and ruddy complexion; hair red or sandy, rather crisp or curly; sharp hazel eyes; a constitution very healthy, and temperament that is decidedly muscular, with full combativeness. A good head, with large perceptives.

The mental conditions conferred by him are boldness and bravery, rendering the mind imperious, versatile, generous, magnanimous, confident, rash, contemptuous, angry, violent, stern, commanding or excited. Under affliction the mind would become cruel, furious, headstrong or turbulent, and very mischievous, with strong inclination to murderous action, arising from rash and impulsive wrath.

The diseases caused by Mars are fevers, smallpox, scarlatina, the plague, carbuncles, headaches, yellow jaundice, fistula, the stone, diseases in the reins and bladder, bad disorders connected with the external generative organs, scalding, cuts and wounds, the shingles, hurts by sharp instruments, blows, and gunshots. In his negative aspect he rules the gall, and in his positive the whole muscular system.

His occupations are those of physician, apothecary, surgeon, soldier, cutler, butcher, barber, tanner, blacksmith, ironmonger, watchmaker, gunsmith, and mechanics generally

His minerals are among others iron, antimony, arsenic, brimstone, and ochre.

His stones are bloodstone, jasper, lodestone, and also all common red stones.

His weather: red clouds, thunder and pestilential air, and also fair weather following unwholesome mist. His wind comes from the west.

His angel is Samael, and his names are Ares, Mavors, Gradivus, Pyrois, &c.

VENUS.

The nature of Venus is temperate, moist, and fortunate; expressive, loving, affectionate, gentle, beautiful, and peaceful. She makes the body somewhat short, but full, well set and fleshy; face round and complexion dark, but lovely; light brown hair; smoothly rolling eyes, well shaped, hazel and sometimes black; amorous looking, dimpled and smiling face, and a beautiful sweet voice; always fond of music and merry meetings. Love of approbation is well developed, and agreeableness very marked.

The mental state due to her influence is cheerful, kind, happy, charitable, well disposed, modest, witty, refined and very amiable. Under affliction, voluptuous, profligate and careless; amorous, but with lack of discrimination; fond of lewd company; small conscience.

Her diseases are infirmities incident to the matrix; sore throat; all venereal diseases and those connected with the urine, genitals, loins and kidneys; diabetes; impotency. She rules the seed and generative system.

Her professions are those of musician, painter, singer,

jeweller, lapidary, seamstress, linen draper, glover, upholsterer, perfumer, &c.

Her minerals are copper, and mixtures of copper or bronze with other metals.

Her stones are the cornelian, sky-blue sapphire, white and red coral, alabaster, the beryl and chrysolite, diamond and all white stones.

Her weather is clear and serene in summer, with rain and snow in winter; her wind is the south, and her temperament languid.

Her angel is Azrael, and her names Hesperus, Lucifer, Aphrodite, Cytheria, Astarte, &c.

MERCURY.

The nature of Mercury is convertible, cold and dry, mercurial and changeable. He makes the body slight, with somewhat long face, arms, and hands, thin nose and lips, scant hair on face, sallow complexion, very dark, with small eyes, black or grey. Good forehead, small legs, and quick walk. Very active, with good intellect. Nervous temperament, with mental disposition.

The mental conditions induce literary or scientific tendencies, with an inclination to study law and physics; the native is active in writing and matters connected with papers and correspondence; is generally nimble and ingenious, and fond of light and easy methods.

His diseases are: all affections of the brain, madness, vertigo, and lethargy; also phthisis, stammerings, and imperfections in the tongue and memory; silly imaginings, dry coughs, snuffling in the nose; hoarseness, affections of the hands and feet; and nearly all nervous complaints.

His professions are those of accountant, clerk, solicitor.

merchant, agent, secretary, messenger, stationer, lawyer, printer, commissioner, teacher, traveller, sculptor, mathematician, orator, philosopher, ambassador, footman, servant, postman, &c.; rogues, thieves, and sharpers have Mercury prominent, but with the luminaries afflicted.

His mineral is quicksilver.

His stones are the topaz, firestone, agate, and stones of mixed colours.

His weather is bright, clear, and dry, with light but shifting breeze.

His angel is Raphael, and his chief name Hermes.

MOON.

The nature of the Moon is phlegmatic, cold, and moist. She is receptive and changeable. She represents a fair stature of variable shape, face generally round, pale complexion, light brown hair, grey eyes, short arms, head, and feet. Generally placid and emotional, with good domestic qualities.

Mental conditions: peace-loving, with strong desires for ease and comfort, variable and changeable, giving a fondness for roving; the native is inclined to discontent, but is generally active.

Her diseases are: colic, dropsy, rheumatic diseases, cold stomach, gout, falling sickness, abscesses, measles, and lunacy; also hurts to the eyes, blindness, and, in women, menstrues and the liver.

Her professions and occupations are those of sailor, midwife, waterman, fisherman, brewer, nurse, fishmonger, letter-carrier, and also all those who cry their wares in the public streets.

Her mineral is silver.

Her stones are selenite and all soft stones.

Her weather is in accordance with the planets she aspects.

Her angel is Gabriel, and her names Cynthia, Diana, Phœbe, Isis, &c.

THE SUN.

The nature of the Sun is hot and dry, constructive, life-giving, and generous. He makes the body large and strong, of full flesh and a ruddy complexion, with large eyes and fair hair (often flaxen), clear voice, and large head. The constitution is good and "vital" in temperament, the native having also full pride and nobility.

His mental conditions are punctuality, a grave manner, a nature honourable in all things, industrious, of noble thoughts, aspiring, and fond of grandeur and power.

His diseases are affections of the heart, arteries, eyes, and the vital organs; swooning, and impurity of breath.

His professions are all positions of trust and authority and those controlling the state and government, such as commander, banker, &c.; also goldsmiths and all artists of dignified purpose.

His mineral is gold.

His stones are the carbuncle, hyacinth, and chrysolite.

His weather: gentle showers in spring; in summer, heat; in autumn, mist; and in winter, rain, and the east wind.

His angel is Michael; his names Osiris, Apollo, &c.

JUPITER.

The nature of Jupiter is electric, hot and moist, sanguine. He is called the greater fortune. He makes the body upright and tall, strong and well proportioned, with large and long feet, oval face, brown and ruddy complexion, fine high forehead; hair soft, light, and brown, with much beard; * in speech sober, in deportment showing and demanding respect.

Mental conditions: magnanimous, religious, affable, cheerful, honourable, just, open, noble, compassionate and benevolent; always steady and sincere, with a hopeful and fortunate disposition.

His diseases are pleurisy, affections of the liver, lungs, ribs and sides, palpitation, quinsy, flatulence, and fevers arising from wind; putrefaction of the blood, and all blood disorders.

His professions are those of judge, minister, lawyer, professor, bishop, priest, cardinal, chancellor, &c., inclining generally to a professional life of some kind as a rule. As shopkeeper, however, the occupation of clothier or woollen-draper is a suitable one.

His mineral is tin.

His stones are the emerald, sapphire, marble, amethyst, and topaz.

His weather is serene, pleasant, and beautiful; his wind is the north.

His angel is Zadkiel, and his names Zeus, Phæton, Vishnu, Thor, &c.

SATURN.

The nature of Saturn is cold and dry, owing to his magnetic nature. He is considered the greater infortune. He makes the body of middle stature, generally a narrow forehead, small eyes, swarthy complexion, often having

* Sagittarius natives, however, are very prone to shave the chin, if not also the side of the face.

downcast look, thin beard and black or very dark hair; broad chest and shoulders, but often having poor legs. The temperament is slightly phlegmatic, but chiefly nervous and bilious.

The mental conditions are grave, melancholy, studious, industrious, patient, contemplative, receptive; when afflicted, repining or resentful, stupid and cunning.

His diseases are those connected with the hearing, also toothache, agues, and all that proceed from cold; consumption, and all complaints arising from fear, rheumatic gout, jaundice, dropsy, &c. He rules the spleen particularly, and the bones.

His occupations are those of agriculturist, bricklayer, miner and collier, potter, carrier, chimney - sweep, dyer, gardener, sexton, undertaker, shoemaker, navvy, scavenger, plumber, estate agent, farmer, builder, tanner, mason, &c.

His minerals are lead, coals, and the dross of metals.

His stones are of the black, sad, and ashy colour, unpolishable and ugly.

His angel is Cassiel, and his names Kronos, Phæon, &c.

URANUS.

The nature of Uranus, the true name of the planet Herschel, is eccentric, electric, and changeable, being a mixture, or essence, of all the planets. He makes the body tall, upright, and of marked features.

The mental conditions are such as to display eccentricity, abruptness, originality, genius, and superior refinement and subtlety of idea.

His diseases are those which are incurable by ordinary methods, such as heart disease, for instance; he causes sudden deaths or accidents.

His professions: electrician, scientist, metaphysician, astrologer, and uncommon professions of every kind, such as antiquarian, researcher, &c.

Herschel or Uranus is a peculiar planet, and, like Saturn, is malefic to the majority of humanity; for only by a knowledge of the inner Astrology can his mission be understood.

The same remarks apply to Neptune.

The *vital parts* having their centre in the heart are governed by the SUN. The *animal portion* in the brain is governed by MERCURY and the MOON, the latter governing the brain organ, and the former the operative, or working part. JUPITER and VENUS govern the *natural part*, which has its seat in the liver and the reins.

Again, the SUN and MARS govern the *life principles* called "prana," while JUPITER rules the *digestive*, and MERCURY the *imaginative* or apprehensive. The MOON represents the *outgoing* power, and SATURN the retentive, or all that which is retained in the body.

The judgment of the horoscope, when it is completed, is the most difficult part of Astrology; and this, of course, depends entirely upon the natural aptitude and the concentrative power of the student. If deficient in the reasoning faculties, his progress will be slow and laborious. But reason alone will not make him proficient; both the perceptive and reflective portions of the brain must be well developed it is true, and lack of development of these organs is one reason why so many fail to become good Astrologers. Those who cannot give a straightforward judgment without referring to some ancient work to aid them in the delineation of the map are as a rule those whose sole attention is occupied with the externals of Astrology, and who have consequently failed to completely master the science. It is essential that the true nature of each planet be thoroughly understood before any attempt is made to judge a nativity. It is also of paramount importance that the value of each aspect, and the strength of position, together with the character of each sign, be known. When these details are all thoroughly apprehended, and their respective values carefully weighed and adjusted in relation to the particular horoscope under discussion, it then becomes necessary to *synthesize* these varying tendencies, to build the several components into one more or less harmonious and complete whole. It is this which is the most difficult part of the study of Astrology, and the one in which most fail; for while the *analytical* faculty is well developed in many of the present day, the *synthetical* is rare. In this sense, therefore, Astrology may be said to be an *art* rather than a science.

As we have progressed through the series, it will have been observed that every effort has been made to simplify the terms and characters employed to convey a knowledge of the science to beginners. Before stepping into deeper waters, the natures of the planets, signs, and aspects must be accurately known and memorized. The absolute necessity for this will readily appear when, farther on, it is seen that complications begin to arise, such as cross-aspects, dignities, &c., an insight into which the student has not as yet been vouchsafed.

There are many systems of judging the map, and each student will gradually evolve his own.

We shall herein adopt a system entirely new and perfectly

simple, and, before erecting the map that we shall judge, the following general rules will be presented :—

MARS is always hot, expansive, and vivacious. It corresponds in the mineral kingdom to iron, this being a key to its nature. As is known, iron has three different states : cast iron, malleable iron, and steel. The latter can be hardened or softened as desired ; tempered, that is, to suit the use to which it is put. In accordance with the same law, the nature of Mars is modified or intensified by whatever aspect it may bear to the superior planets. It will, therefore, be reasonable if we consider Mars as the indicator or representative of the passions, and its *nature* may be summed up in one word—FORCE.

VENUS is always temperate, receptive, and calm. Her metal is copper, which is malleable, soft, and remarkably ductile. In the human system she represents the sensations and all interior feeling. In all the varying phases of personal emotions, her *nature* may be expressed in the word—LOVE.

MERCURY is convertible, changeable, and mobile. Mercury or quicksilver is the only known metal liquid at ordinary temperatures. It unites readily with the other metals (except iron), and is sometimes used for extracting gold and silver from their ores ; also (when united with *tin*, Jupiter's metal) for silvering mirrors, thus making it a reflector. In the human system it represents the nerves, which convey sensation to the brain, and it must always be looked to to determine the condition of the mind. The one word which expresses its *nature* is—MEDIATOR.

The MOON is moist, cold, and transient. Her metal is silver, which is ductile and malleable, and which is known as the most perfect conductor of heat and electricity. The

Moon represents the functional portion. She is the collector and receiver of influences governing all externals; therefore, in one word we consider her the *symbol* of — the PERSONALITY.

The quality of the SUN is always that of vital heat, he being the symbol of an abstract principle, or that which we call "spirit." Gold is the metal ruled by the SUN, and it is remarkable for its ductility and malleability, it being possible to hammer one ounce into 100 square feet of leaf. In Astrology, the Sun is the planet representing the highest, or rather the central, point, and in all physical matters we cannot get higher than the Sun, which in man governs the heart. Perhaps the word which best conveys to the mind its *nature* is—INDIVIDUALITY.

JUPITER also represents heat, electricity, and moisture. His mineral is tin, which is used extensively in combination with other metals, and is, moreover, very soft and malleable, greatly resembling gold in the latter respect, though inferior to the latter in ductility. Jupiter rules the blood and liver, and governs all pure motive, compassion, benevolence, and sincerity. To come under his influence is to LIVE, since he is the planet of hope, and also of good fortune; for hope brings success. In a word, he is in his *nature* the—HIGHER MIND.

SATURN is always cold, dry, and magnetic or receptive. His metal is lead, which is dull and heavy, and lacks tenacity. Saturn governs the bones of the human structure —the concrete, hard and heavy portion of man's make-up and all which tends to densify or crystallize into set forms. We have therefore placed all the selfish and self-centring habits under the domain of this planet; and dividing the mind into two portions, Saturn is placed as ruler of the lower or conventional and concrete mind, representing—LIMITATION.

It now becomes necessary to consider whether we should bring URANUS and NEPTUNE within the purview of these lessons. The Chaldeans do not appear to have made use of these planets, or if they did we have no trace of the symbols, for they are not mentioned in any ancient works that we have seen. But experience, which alone must be our teacher, proves that both planets play a most important part in our modern Astrology, and why this should be so can easily be seen by those who understand the objects of this science.

As we evolve, fresh powers lie open before us, faculties that have been latent begin to awaken, and as Astrologers we perceive that Uranus is of the greatest importance, since he governs all that is original and independent, or above the limited and cramped vision of ordinary "orthodox" minds. The Son of Uranus is independent of the opinions of those who are bound by conventional customs and old stereotyped notions. Without this planet we should not be able to account for the circumstance that some can undertake the study of Astrology, while others, equally keen of intellect, fail entirely. The influence of Uranus is the quintessence of all the planets beneath him, and, irrespective of any others, an aspect to Uranus will always be very markedly manifest. When well aspected and above the earth he gives remarkable intuition and originality of style and expression, endowing one with the ability to express as much in one sentence as the newspaper editor with a well aspected Mercury could manage in a whole column. The perception of

TAURUS.

(Sign ruler ♀)   *(Decanate rulers ♀ ☿ ♄)*

1°— 5°. Middle stature, dark complexion, generally black hair, small blue eyes. *Characteristics :* solemn
♀ -   and determined; sometimes thoughtful, but discontented.

5°—10°. Shorter stature than 1° to 5°, more compact, full face, swarthy and somewhat ill conditioned.
♀ +   *Characteristics :* shifty and unsettled ; somewhat desponding, and peevish.

10°—15°. Short stature, sullen appearance, features poor and rather disagreeable, a tendency to corpulence, scanty hair. *Characteristics :* envious,
☿ +   indifferent, often lazy and inactive ; undesirable companions, ill-natured and unfeeling.

15°—20°. Taller in stature than the former, more pleasant in features, a good form—the opposite of the foregoing — often good looking, rather fair
☿ -   complexion, light brown hair. *Characteristics :* affectionate, good and faithful disposition ; very receptive nature.

20°—25°. Poor or medium stature, sanguine complexion, often lymphatic, dark eyes. *Characteristics :*
♄ -   not good, too much subtlety, often turned to improper account ; as a rule, conscientiousness is small. It is an unfortunate portion.

25°—30°. Good form, nicely developed, dark complexion,
♄ +   black hair. *Characteristics :* somewhat loose, and deceptive.

GEMINI

(Sign ruler ☿)   *(Decanate rulers ☿ ♀ ♄)*

1°— 5°. Slender build, rather fair hair, dark complexion, shifty gait. *Characteristics:* somewhat conceited and given to hypocrisy, often dishonest, and overreaching.

☿ +

5°—10°. Good complexion, fair stature, light hair, jovial face. *Characteristics:* somewhat vain, fond of approbation, and careful of self-interests, but easily influenced.

☿ −

10°—15°. Rather short, very dark, soft features, ruddy complexion. *Characteristics:* bombastic and over-bearing, sometimes sarcastic, and very talkative.

♀ −

15°—20°. Larger stature, clear complexion, brilliant eyes, refined appearance. *Characteristics:* free, active, impulsive and witty, courageous, and intellectual.

♀ +

20°—25°. Well built, rather slender, dark hair and eyes, narrow palish brown face. *Characteristics:* diplomatic, sensuous.

♄ +

25°—30°. Well formed and good features, pale complexion, sheeny hair. *Characteristics:* bold, obliging, with tact and talent well blended.

♄ −

———

Gemini on the whole generally indicates one who is tall, very active, with hazel eyes, and dark complexion. Quick and sprightly walker; very intellectual.

CANCER

(Sign ruler ☽)   *(Decanate rulers ☽ ♂ ♃)*

1°— 5°. Middle stature, full and fleshy, dark brown hair.
  ☽ –   *Characteristics :* plenty of tact, fully awake, but rather suspicious.

5°—10°. Small stature and face, good forehead, dark hair and complexion, bluish eyes. *Characteristics :*
  ☽ +   rather vain, fully conscious of abilities, fond of romance and adventure.

10°—15°. Average stature, black hair, small nose and pale thin face, shrill voice. *Characteristics :* tena-
  ♂ +   cious nature; combative, but inclined to be sad, and selfish.

15°—20°. Very thin, awkward build, dark complexion, black hair, grey eyes. *Characteristics :* desponding
  ♂ –   temperament, obstinate, often self-willed.

20°—25°. Thin and slender, not well made, features some-what out of proportion, brown hair. *Charac-
  ♄ –   teristics :* plenty of self-esteem, and given to foolish acts; often very talkative.

25°—30°. Short stature, long face, often freckled, large eyes and nose, small chin, inclined to corpulence.
  ♄ +   *Characteristics :* shrewd, active, often high-spirited, thoughtful and contemplative; to be relied upon, having much patience.

––––––––––

The general indications of Cancer are crab-like, small features, dark hair and a pale round face, inclined to be fleshy. Very magnetic and tenacious.

LEO

(Sign ruler ☉)   *(Decanate rulers ☉ ♃ ♂)*

1°— 5°.   Broad, well formed, but not tall stature; fine
features, brown hair. *Characteristics:* rather
☉ +   daring, imperious and bombastic; highly magnetic.

5°—10°.   Middle stature, fine clear skin, light hair and
eyes. *Characteristics:* kind and generous, and
☉ –   very attractive; willing and enduring, but with
small self-esteem.

10°—15°.   Broad stature, dark hair and eyes, full beard,
pale complexion. *Characteristics:* good dis-
♃ –   position, honourable and frank, with full discretion; very generous.

15°—20°.   Slender, inclined to be tall, light hair, pale
complexion, good forehead, well developed.
♃ +   *Characteristics:* diplomatic, ingenious.

20°—25°.   Well proportioned, fine manly stature, full face,
sharp eyes. *Characteristics:* very sincere, up-
♂ +   right and noble, fearless and generous;
splendid vitality.

25°—30°.   Slender build, dark eyes and hair, good, well-
proportioned upper part, with short legs.
Characteristics: diplomatic, impulsive, generous
♂ –   and sincere in friendship. The powerful fixed
star Regulus is in this portion.

———————

Leo gives a fine body, full carriage, quick sight, a
courageous nature; very aspiring, and confident; generous
to a fault.

VIRGO

(Sign ruler ☿) *(Decanate rulers ☿ ♄ ♀)*

1°— 5°. Tall and slender, brown eyes and hair, good
☿ – intellectual forehead. *Characteristics:* mentally
proud, with full tact and subtlety.

5°—10°. Tall stature, light brown hair and eyes, good
☿ + complexion. *Characteristics:* honest, sincere
and refined.

10°—15°. Full stature, blue-grey eyes, light curling hair,
good features and clear complexion. *Charac-*
♄ + *teristics:* amiable, refined, pleasant and agreeable; scientific tastes.

15°—20°. Tall and slender, round face, good forehead;
dark mercurial eyes. *Characteristics:* fond of
♄ – the arts and sciences, rich and fluent of speech;
very prudent and discreet.

20°—25°. Tall, long thin face, high cheek-bones, black
eyes, thin lips, broad nose and nostrils.
Characteristics: affable, intellectual, bright and
♀ – sincere; a good speaker; anxious to do good;
often serving others.

25°—30°. A good form and sprightly, fair complexion.
Characteristics: artistic ability; materialistic
♀ + in tendency; rather too anxious in relation
to others' affairs.

Virgo inclines to a tall and slender form; ruddy complexion, dark brown hair; often a shrill voice; strong
business tendencies.

LIBRA

(*Sign ruler* ♀)   (*Decanate rulers* ♀ ♄ ☿)

1°— 5°.

♀ +

Rather tall, with oval face, pale complexion, grey eyes, auburn hair; very good looking. *Characteristics:* sincere, mutable, kind and affable, fluent in speech, of good understanding, and generally a favourite.

5°—10°.

♀ –

Tall and corpulent, with clear complexion, blue eyes and light hair. *Characteristics:* serious and discreet.

10°—15°.

♄ –

Middle stature, dark complexion, grey eyes, good forehead, dark hair, attractive features. *Characteristics:* thoughtful, studious, serious, shrewd, and diplomatic.

15°—20°.

♄ +

Slender build, with clear complexion and greenish-grey eyes; very magnetic, and of permanent beauty. *Characteristics:* grave, just, prudent and thoughtful, with scientific tendencies.

20°—25°.

☿ +

Good form, fine fresh complexion, and dark-blue eyes; a beautiful person. *Characteristics:* a good disposition, kind and generous to all; very scientific.

25°—30°.

☿ –

Tall, and of splendid form; very graceful and beautiful, with light brown eyes and hair. *Characteristics:* noble, virtuous and honourable; one to be admired and respected.

Libra gives a good form generally, fair and beautiful skin, and blue eyes. First half dark, last portion fair. Very good looking.

SCORPIO

(Sign ruler ♂)   *(Decanate rulers ♂ ♃ ☽)*

1°— 5°. Middle stature, inclining to be short, fair complexion and full round face, sometimes ruddy.

♂ — *Characteristics :* of full habit, generous and pleasant; highly magnetic.

5°—10°. Short, firm, stout build; reddish or chestnut hair, quick dark-grey eyes. *Characteristics :*

♂ + generous, fond of the mystical, of good parts; strong will.

10°—15°. Middle stature, well proportioned, and of fair and open countenance; fair hair, and eyes of greyish colour. *Characteristics :* thoughtful,

♃ + discreet, generous, and of good disposition; fond of art and science, creditable in ambition, and of fixed purpose.

15°—20°. Slender build, with dark hair and sunburnt appearance. *Characteristics :* a splendid nature,

♃ — noble and just, fond of all the arts and sciences, especially music and painting.

20°—25°. Small stature, well proportioned, oval and pale face, good features. *Characteristics :* an artist,

☽ — of good disposition; often very fond of the opposite sex.

25°—30°. Well made but generally short person, reddish hair and ruddy complexion. *Characteristics :*

☽ + just, of good character, but at times too easily led into the pleasures of the senses.

Scorpio gives a strong, robust body; generally dark; often reserved and mystical; generally a very strong will.

SAGITTARIUS

(Sign ruler ♃)   *(Decanate rulers ♃ ♂ ☉)*

1°— 5°.

♃ +

Tall, broad shoulders, long face and good forehead, keen brown eyes, and light brown hair; complexion often freckled; active walk. *Characteristics :* sincere, intellectual, of good disposition; a careful speaker, generous and hopeful.

5°—10°.

♃ —

Middle stature, and a well-formed body; more fair than the former, light hair, dark eyes; *Characteristics :* active, religious, thoughtful and contemplative.

10°—15°.

♂ —

Shorter stature, with full body; generally very fair, with small mouth and greyish eyes. *Characteristics :* active temperament, fond of travelling and adventure, well disposed and somewhat generous; great vitality.

15°—20°.

♂ +

Full stature, rather heavy build, full features and long face, grey eyes, brown hair. *Characteristics :* not favourable, rather vain and pretentious, apeing that to which they cannot fully give expression.

20°—25°.

☉ +

Slim build, about, or a little above, medium height, well set; full motive temperament; rather pleasant countenance. *Characteristics :* rather fickle and given to changes; thoughtful, but often rash.

25°—30°.

☉ —

Rather tall, with plump features, good complexion, and dark-grey eyes. *Characteristics :* sincere and faithful; inclined to be hasty, but well intentioned.

CAPRICORN

(Sign ruler ♄ *)*   *(Decanate rulers* ♄ ♀ ☿ *)*

1°— 5°. Tall and slender, well-formed features, between
♄ -   dark and fair. *Characteristics:* noble, very
         just, sincere and kind; of good thoughts and
         intentions, and fully to be trusted.

5°—10. Small stature, with longish face but good and
        pleasant features; small self-esteem. *Char-*
♄ +   *acteristics:* generous and free, sincere, just,
        and to be depended upon; a good speaker.

10°—15°. Muscular, of full stature and somewhat com-
          manding appearance. *Characteristics:* of in-
♀ +   dependent mood, yet well disposed; plenty of
          tact and diplomacy.

15°—20°. Shorter stature, but of good appearance; clear
          skin, light brown hair. *Characteristics:* of
♀ -   lively temperament and successful manners,
          but often imposed upon.

20°—25°. Fine stature, noble carriage, good appearance,
          and splendid features; more fair than dark.
☿ -   *Characteristics:* free and generous spirit,
          seeking good before evil; very thoughtful.

25°—30°. Well proportioned, middle stature, fair com-
          plexion, light hair. *Characteristics:* ambitious
☿ +   and aspiring to lead; often fond of pleasure.

Capricorn gives a bony structure, more tall than short,
with generally a long face and black or brown hair and
scanty beard. Natives of Capricorn are generally sincere
and thoughtful; often good politicians.

AQUARIUS

(*Sign ruler* ♄)   (*Decanate rulers* ♄ ☿ ♀)

1°— 5°.   Tall, brown complexion, and dark eyes.
♄ +   *Characteristics:* amiable, easy disposition, yet self-willed; liable to many temptations, subtle.

5°—10°.   Dark complexion and small features; not tall.
♄ −   *Characteristics:* easily led, fond of pleasure, and often falling into uncertain habits; very unreliable.

10°—15°.   Tall stature, with clear complexion, sharp bright eyes, thin features, and brown hair. *Characteristics:* quick, thoughtful, fond of discourse;
☿ −   active nature.

15°—20°.   Middle stature, dark complexion, small dark eyes, good forehead. *Characteristics:* mercurial nature, ingenious, and with good opinion of
☿ +   personal abilities.

20°—25°.   Clear complexion, medium stature, well-formed thin features, grey eyes, and light hair.
♀ +   *Characteristics:* fond of change; anxious to learn; a good speaker.

25°—30°.   Full stature; good complexion; handsome type of person. *Characteristics:* changeable and
♀ −   fond of ease, yet well disposed.

Aquarius as a rule gives a good, robust middle stature. very fair hair generally, sometimes flaxen; a good honest nature, but difficult to understand.

PISCES

(Sign ruler ♃)   (Decanate rulers ♃ ☽ ♂)

1°— 5°. Tall, broad shoulders, heavy build, sunken eyes, dark hair. *Characteristics:* a subtle disposition, fond of study; mediumistic and often inclined to spiritualism.

♃ –

5°—10°. Heavy and large bony stature; brown hair. *Characteristics:* thoughtful, studious, fond of the arts and sciences; very patient.

♃ +

10°—15°. Short stature, with good features, fair; face oval. *Characteristics:* just, upright and well disposed, ever seeking good.

☽ +

15°—20°. Middle stature, dark bushy hair, soft features; often freckled. *Characteristics:* a good student, sincere and faithful, and of excellent judgment.

☽ –

20°—25°. Well proportioned and muscular; chestnut hair, grey eyes. *Characteristics:* pleasant, generous, and free; often a strong character.

♂ –

25°—30°. Small stature, ruddy complexion, hard dry features, dark hair. *Characteristics:* bold, combative, and somewhat conceited.

♂ +

———

Pisces usually gives a short plump stature, full watery eyes; complexion more dark than fair; disposition good, easy and generous; often much inclined to spiritualism; mediumistic tendencies.

CHAPTER XV

IN the first part of these instructions we laid stress upon the necessity of first knowing the nature of the planets and of the twelve signs before attempting the study of the horoscope as such. The reason for this will now be seen as we proceed to examine the twelve divisions called the houses.

When dealing with the planets, we showed how the dot in the centre of the circle was the energizing point out of which all sprang. The expansion of the circle around the dot will serve us for the outer ring of the horoscope, inside of which the planets will have their limitations, the earth being the central point around which the planets move in their apparent diurnal revolutions. Now if we extend from the centre lines of communication to the outer ring, we can imagine this dot as the nucleus out of which all will grow, it forming the embryo of all that is to be of the man. In the solar system it is the Sun, and so in a human being it is the centre of himself, each radiation being a manifestation, or expression, of his powers. Astrology is regarded from the standpoint of the earth as centre when dealing with humanity in manifestation, because the body is the focus into which the principles play These forces or attributes of the Sun must needs have a vehicle or body through which to act, or their value cannot be felt and realized; and this is why modern Astrology is based upon the zodiac surrounding the earth,* and not

* The zodiac of the *signs* ♈, ♉, &c.

that of the Sun.* We are human, and thus under law, governed by planetary influences. When we break away from this limitation, then planetary law, as enunciated in Astrology as we know it, can hold us no longer. But until we have done with the material world, its laws must bind us; and to understand its laws we must first understand the body and the senses. Pursued in this way, a true knowledge of the science comes quickly.

Now let us start to build up our map from these lines of radiation from the centre; for this will give us a speedy knowledge of each house as marked off by the lines. We will commence with a triple line flashing out representing the physical and material houses, *corresponding* to what are called the Earthy signs, as follows:—

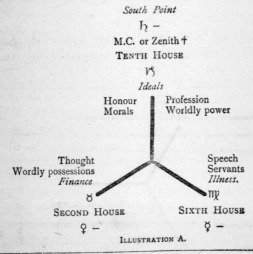

South Point

♄ −

M.C. or Zenith †
TENTH HOUSE

♑

Ideals

Honour
Morals

Profession
Worldly power

Thought
Wordly possessions
Finance

Speech
Servants
Illness.

♉
SECOND HOUSE

♍
SIXTH HOUSE

♀ −

☿ −

ILLUSTRATION A.

---

* The zodiac of the *constellations* ♈, ♉, &c.

† *Medium Cœli*, or midheaven: the opposite point is the I.C. or *Imum Cœli.*

Then, following with the house allied to the watery triplicity from below, we shall have the emotional and sensational points, or what is termed the astral, or psychic.

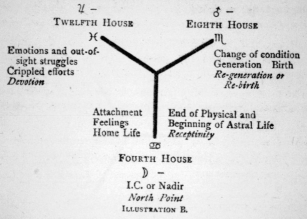

ILLUSTRATION B.

Then culminating in the West we have houses corresponding to the airy triplicity, the points representing the mental conditions, or what is finally to be the Soul :—

ILLUSTRATION C.

Finally, we shall have those that represent the fiery triplicity, culminating in the East, or the Ascendant, as a focus of the whole in outward expression, or that which is the real man on earth, as follows:—

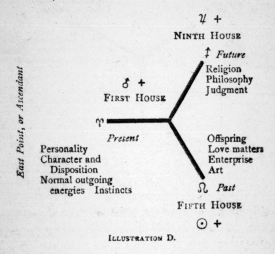

ILLUSTRATION D.

Now, taking the whole, we shall have the complete horoscope of twelve houses, forming a round map, as may be easily seen by placing illustration B upon A, then C upon these two, and finally D upon the whole. We shall now by way of change use the square map to illustrate this, as there are many who use square maps, and it is necessary to be acquainted with them.

It will be seen that each house has been given a quality which corresponds to the signs, and the planets ruling them, in their natural order from Aries to Pisces: *and this nature they always retain irrespective of the signs that may fall upon each house when the horoscope of an individual is erected; but only to the minor extent of forming The Environment.*

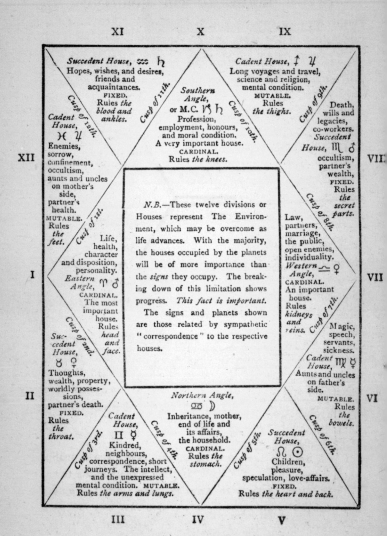

XI X IX

Succedent House, ♒ ♄
Hopes, wishes, and desires, friends and acquaintances.
FIXED.
Rules *the blood and ankles.*

Cusp of 11th.

Southern Angle,
or M.C. ♑ ♄
Profession, employment, honours, and moral condition.
A very important house.
CARDINAL.
Rules *the knees.*

Cusp of 10th.

Cadent House, ♐ ♃
Long voyages and travel, science and religion, mental condition.
MUTABLE.
Rules *the thighs.*

Cusp of 9th.

Cadent House ♓ ♃
Enemies, sorrow, confinement, occultism, aunts and uncles on mother's side, partner's health.
MUTABLE.
Rules *the feet.*

Cusp of 12th.

Death, wills and legacies, co-workers.
Succedent House, ♏ ♂
occultism, partner's wealth,
FIXED.
Rules *the secret parts.*

Cusp of 8th.

XII

Life, health, character and disposition, personality.
Eastern Angle, ♈ ♂
CARDINAL.
The most important house.
Rules *head and face.*

Cusp of 1st.

N.B.—These twelve divisions or Houses represent The Environment, which may be overcome as life advances. With the majority, the houses occupied by the planets will be of more importance than the *signs* they occupy. The breaking down of this limitation shows progress. *This fact is important.* The signs and planets shown are those related by sympathetic "correspondence" to the respective houses.

Law, partners, marriage, the public, open enemies, individuality.
Western Angle, ♎ ♀
CARDINAL.
An important house.
Rules *kidneys and veins.*

VII

Cusp of 7th.

Succedent House, ♉ ♀
Thoughts, wealth, property, worldly possessions, partner's death.
FIXED.
Rules *the throat.*

Cusp of 2nd.

Magic, speech, servants, sickness.
Cadent House, ♍ ☿
Aunts and uncles on father's side.
MUTABLE.
Rules *the bowels.*

Cusp of 6th.

II VI

Cadent House,
♊ ☿
Kindred, neighbours, correspondence, short journeys. The intellect, and the unexpressed mental condition. MUTABLE.
Rules *the arms and lungs.*

Cusp of 3rd.

Northern Angle, ♋ ☽
Inheritance, mother, end of life and its affairs, the household.
CARDINAL.
Rules *the stomach.*

Cusp of 4th.

Succedent House, ♌ ☉
Children, pleasure, speculation, love-affairs.
FIXED.
Rules *the heart and back.*

Cusp of 5th.

III IV V

We shall now take into consideration the twelve houses, as marked off in the divisions of the illustrative map. In each house or division we have placed the leading characteristics, the whole embracing that which constitutes the environment of the PERSONALITY, which has its beginning in the First House, commonly called the Ascendant. The range of this portion takes in the life, energy, constitution, character and disposition.

This is why the rising sign is of such importance, and why it needs the most careful study; for it is in this division that the whole of the life will focus itself. We have summed up this house as The Personality, of the nature of Mars and Aries. We may think of it as a focus through which the Life forces pour, and we shall immediately require to know something of the life or essence that is pouring through. To begin with, we may think of its underlying substance as comparable to the colour Red, and in accordance with the nature of the other colours that we find mixing with the red, so we shall be able to form a judgment as to its quality. In Chapter XIII. we gave to each of the planets a metal, thus conveying at once an idea of density. To Mars we gave iron; therefore this house will also represent in its totality rough iron, Mars being the ruler of Aries, which is the first house in the natural order of the signs, and so the foundation of the nature of the first house in the horoscope. This rough iron we may think of as the substance upon which we shall have to work to extract its real and general meaning. Every schoolboy knows what a useful metal crude iron may become; it may be reduced by intense heat to the consistency of dough, and then from its impure state of pig iron may be con-

I

verted into steel, which can be tempered to any degree of elasticity or hardness. In the same way, if we were to consider the very first group of human personalities coming under the domain of horoscopy, we might imagine them as being represented by iron in its most crude condition, gradually, as the successive human races evolved through countless years, becoming purer and stronger, *tempered* and *refined*, as it were, by experience.

There are three conditions of this metal (as there are three states of all things), cast iron, malleable iron, and steel, and so we shall assuredly have three groups of persons coming under this sign Aries—and by the same law the first house—this depending upon the decanate of the sign ascending, each 10 degrees having a special virtue in themselves.* We may also extend these three qualities as follows :—(1) The general character of the house from the sign rising upon the Ascendant, (2) the ruling planet, and (3) the planets, if any, placed in the Ascendant; each governing in their respective order of importance as above. We may think of the cusp of this house as a radiating point from which will flow a current of life—strong or weak, in accordance with the rising sign and its ruler, or the planets we may find located therein ; and from this we shall judge the quality of the life, and, to some extent, the character and disposition.

We can apply this rule to each of the twelve houses. With the majority of humanity we shall find that these twelve houses indicate the environment in which they *always* move ; but occasionally we shall find some to whom this

---

* In the same way, the first house itself may be divided into three parts. Each of these, however, will consist of 10 degrees of *oblique ascension*, and not of 10 degrees of the zodiac ; the former being either less or more than the latter, according to the latitude of the birth place and the S.T. of birth. See "The House of the Horoscope" in *Astrology for All, Part II.*

rule will not apply, since they break away from this limitation, and so come under the signs in their natural order, irrespective of the houses.

We shall first deal with the houses apart from the signs until we have made our ideas clear, when we shall advance to the general maps including both orders. For a time we shall adopt a system of twin contrast maps to illustrate fully the meaning of all statements made, a system never yet attempted, and one which we hope will prove interesting, useful, and instructive. The two first maps illustrate the vitality as springing from the first house. In the first map the houses are *numbered*, to prevent any chance of error.

The student will be well advised to pause before turning over the page, and make up his mind *how* he is going to study the contrast that is there presented. If he is wise, he will first turn his attention to Contrast Map No. 1, and —(without looking further to read a word of what is said about it)—STUDY IT WELL: that is, he will *fix in his mind* the planetary positions and aspects; commencing with the Ascendant, Moon, and Sun, and proceeding to the Lord of the Ascendant, Mercury, Venus, Mars, &c., in due order When he feels that he really knows these, the house, sign, and (approximate) degree occupied by each planet, and the cusps of the Ascendant and M.C., then he should turn to p. 134, and read what is there said about *this* map [leaving the other one altogether out of consideration for the present]. He will find that his preliminary concentration will make the remarks there given at least ten times more useful and illuminating than if he had read them either before studying the map, or after confusing his mind by looking at both maps.

This procedure, it is true, calls for a certain amount of self-restraint, for it is natural to wish to run on ahead, but the added insight gained will more than compensate for this.

CONTRAST MAP, No. 1.

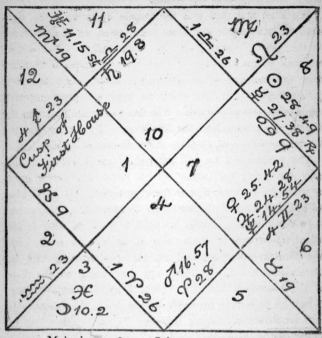

Male, born 4.8 P.M., July 21, 1894, London.

Decl.	Asp.	Decl.	Asp.
⊙ 20° N	☌ ☿ : ▭ ☽	♂ 4° N	☍ ♄
☽ 10° S	▭ ☿ : ▭ ⊙	♃ 23° N	☌ ♀ : ▭ ⛢
☿ 16° N	☌ ⊙ : ▭ ☽	♄ 5° S	☍ ♂
♀ 22° N	☌ ♃ : ▭ ⛢	⛢ 15° S	▭ ♀ : ▭ ♃

4 Common.	4 Water.
4 Cardinal.	4 Air.
1 Fixed.	1 Fire.

4 Negative.
5 Positive.

CONTRAST MAP, No. 2.

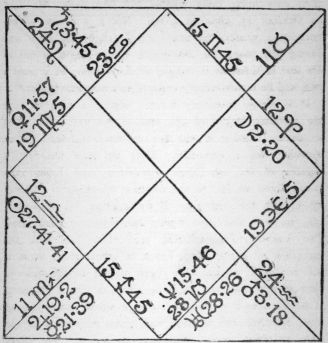

Male, born 3 A.M. October 21, 1828, Ecclefechan, Scotland.

Decl.	Asp.	Decl.	Asp.
☉ 1°	□ ♅	♂ 22°	☍ ♄: ∠ ☽
☽ 2°	⚼ ☉: △ ♃: △ ☿	♃ 17°	☌ ☿: △ ☽
☿ 21°	☌ ♃: △ ☽: ✶ ♅	♄ 20°	☍ ♂: □ ☽
♀ 7°	☍ ☽: ✶ ♃	♅ 21°	P. ☿: ☌ ♂

4 Fixed.		2 Earth.	
2 Cardinal.		2 Air.	
2 Common.		1 Fire.	
3 Water.	3 Positive.	5 Negative.	

In case No. 1 the vitality was exceedingly low, the child only living three months and four days. He died on October 25, 1894, at 5 P.M. No. 2 is a case of extraordinary vitality, the native being (1896) still alive and having just passed his sixty-eighth year. He is so full of life that at times he is obliged to throw some of it into a tree, and he is now usefully engaged as a magnetic healer.*

It is always necessary before judging a map to note the probable length of life, and in the case of a child to decide whether it will live or not; therefore, let us consider No. 1 especially. Here we have the first 5 degrees of the sign Sagittarius rising, and Jupiter the ruling planet we find in the common sign Gemini, afflicted by Uranus, the destroyer. If we examine the map carefully we shall find poor vitality borne out in many ways. The luminaries are afflicting each other, and with the exception of Jupiter and Venus in conjunction, there is not one good aspect. We were present at the time of birth of this child, and on being asked to give a judgment as to the length of life, we stated it would barely exceed three months: this opinion was given in writing at the time, to which several witnesses can testify. We based our judgment upon the following consideration:—

The Moon, ruler of the eighth, is applying to the affliction by sesqui-quadrate of the Sun and Mercury in the eighth, the midway point of these two being 28° 15′, to the □ of which point the Moon moving 1 degree per month † would arrive in three months.

---

* At time of printing first edition: he died March 1905—see *Modern Astrology*, vol. ii., *New Series* (p. 198).

† The "direction" of 1 day = 1 year has been mentioned before; the ☽ moves about 12 degrees per day, and at this rate, of course, 1 degree is

The child died at the age mentioned while on a short journey (☽ in 3rd) to the doctor. Now if the map be read by way of signs, Mars is found in the first sign Aries, and in opposition to Saturn; Jupiter is in the third sign, afflicted by Uranus from the eighth sign, Scorpio. Thus the testimony of the houses is borne out by the signs, and therefore it was not difficult to judge that the child could not live. On the day of death Saturn was in square aspect to the Sun, and the Moon in Virgo in square to Jupiter, all these assisting to reduce the vitality to its lowest ebb.

Now let us study the Contrast Map No. 2. This gentleman is well known for his marvellous healing power and remarkable vitality. The sign Virgo ascends, and Mercury, the ruling planet, is placed in Scorpio, in conjunction with Jupiter, applying to the sextile of Uranus and entirely free from affliction, in the third house,—the natural home of Mercury. Not only has the native splendid vitality (☉ in ♎), which fills him with hope and gives a buoyant and healthy love of life, but also wonderful sympathy. The contrast between the two maps is very marked, and they should be well studied.

In taking a general survey of the life, we must consider the Moon equally with the first house; for she is ruler of the natural fourth (♋), the negative point through which the whole magnetism outpours, and is so intimately related with the first as to need almost the same amount of attention with regard to the life; for what is signified by the first, as the beginning, is taken up by the fourth, the

equivalent to one month. [For fuller information as to the various methods of "direction" in use the reader is referred to *The Progressed Horoscope* (see advertisement at end of book).]

end. It is this which makes the Moon such an important factor, not only with regard to the first four years of a child, but to the whole life. The Sun, however, must always be considered as a giver of life, and the amount of vitality possessed must be judged best by studying the Sun and the Moon, the principal factors—first separately, and then in their relationship to each other.

There are certain points in the twelve houses that are called hylegiacal places. These are : From 5 degrees below the seventh house to 5 degrees beyond the cusp of the eighth (which is equivalent to saying from 25 degrees ♍ to 5 degrees ♏ in the natural order of the signs): again, the opposite points, from 5 degrees above the Ascendant to 25 degrees below : the whole of the ninth, tenth, and eleventh houses also are considered hylegiacal.

The ancients considered the Sun hyleg when in these positions if the native was born between sunrise and sunset, and the Moon when there if birth took place between sunset and sunrise. If neither of the luminaries was found in these positions, then the ascending degree was taken as hyleg. But these latter rules we do not consider of much importance, as we shall point out when we come to deal with the eighth house and death. Sufficient has been said to show that the Sun, Moon, and Ascendant are the three points to consider with regard to vitality, when judging the map.

CHAPTER XVI

CHARACTER AND DISPOSITION

THE next important matter to consider is the character and disposition: and without the slightest hesitation we say that this is the most important consideration in the whole of the judgment, for upon it rests the future action of the native. We are constantly building character, and our present character is the outcome of our past. It is our character that influences our conduct toward the opportunities that life affords, even as it shapes the motives for our actions. If we are noble-minded, then all our motives and actions will tend toward nobility; if sordid, then only those things that are sordid in nature can attract us.

The whole of our life is coloured by our character. For if evil in nature, then we seek for the evil; but if good and pure, then only toward that which is good can we gravitate. We view everything in accordance with our character and disposition first, and the former is the root out of which the whole has sprung. This root is the result of either our primeval ignorance, or the knowledge gathered from *experience* in previous lives. Each day we are moulding our future character by the various impressions, sensations, and experiences that our environment affords, the mind and senses being the means whereby we are impressed, the character having stored in it the sum total of all past experiences.

In studying character and disposition, all the planets will play a more or less important part, but chief amongst them all will be the nature of the sign upon the Ascendant, its ruler, and the Sun and Moon.

The rising sign may be considered as the natural or permanent indicator of the character, and this will give twelve distinct types, briefly summarized as follows :—

♈ ARIES. Frank and outspoken, combative, generous, assertive and impulsive; intuitive, yet fond of reason and argument.

♉ TAURUS. Dogmatic and obstinate, fearless and strong-willed, patient and determined; affectionate, but sullen and secretive.

♊ GEMINI. Dualistic and restless, intellectual and sensational, nervous and irritable; yet kind and generous.

♋ CANCER. Reserved and sensitive, sympathetic and tenacious, impatient yet persistent; impressionable and emotional.

♌ LEO. Firm and self-controlling, persevering and ambitious; faithful, noble and generous, and intuitive in regard to spiritual matters.

♍ VIRGO. Retiring and discriminative yet ingenious and active; mercurial and inventive, thoughtful and speculative.

♎ LIBRA. Sensitive and compassionate, inspirational and perceptive; yielding, amalgamative, just and generous.

♏ SCORPIO   Reserved,   determined   and   tenacious,

secretive, wise and discreet, firm and proud;
resentful of injuries.

♐ SAGITTARIUS. Active and enterprising, frank and
honest, generous and sincere; impressionable yet
introspective, demonstrative.

♑ CAPRICORN. Melancholic, ambitious, penetrative and
receptive; persistent and steady, inspirational
and politically inclined.

♒ AQUARIUS. Intellectual and retentive, studious and
thoughtful, diffusive and versatile; yet ever
ingenious and artistic.

♓ PISCES. Emotional and secretive, patient and meditative, kind and generous; imitative and receptive,
patient and peace-loving.

The ruling planet will then need consideration. First
as to *house* position; next as to *sign* position; then as to
its *aspects*. Also, any planet that may come in the
Ascendant should be considered, being regarded as a tem-
porary lord of the Ascendant, so to speak, to be in due
time "disposed" of, to use a technical expression, by the
planet ruling the *sign* on the Ascendant. For instance, in
Map 2 we have ♀ rising near the Ascendant, disposed of
by ☿.

The general natures of the planets may be summarized
as follows :—

♂ MARS. Impulsive, courageous, aggressive, active,
sensual, perceptive, impatient, contentious and
generous—or rather, lavish.

♀ VENUS. Loving, amiable, feeling, affectionate, charitable, yet sensuous and fond of pleasure, artistic,
and social.

☿ MERCURY. Mercurial, depending chiefly upon aspects to other planets or to the Moon, but in the main imaginative, quick, studious, sharp, witty, persuasive, logical, and oratorical. Being "convertible," however, everything depends upon how this planet is aspected or placed.

☉ SUN. Noble, generous, faithful and sincere, ambitious and proud, governing.

☽ MOON. Receptive and mutable, impressionable, changeable, yet refined and ingenious.

♃ JUPITER. Generous, noble and sincere, compassionate and religious, courteous, just, honourable, prudent and faithful.

♄ SATURN. Perceptive, imaginative and apprehensive, economical, reserved, constant, patient, suspicious, nervous, timid, melancholic, laborious, reflective, and innately chaste.

♅ URANUS. Original, abrupt, erratic, romantic, bohemian, of a metaphysical turn of mind and antiquarian tastes.

♆ NEPTUNE. Psychic, emotional, romantic, plastic and dreamy, innately mystical and indifferent to worldly matters.

It must be remembered that an aspect of one planet to another will transfer some of its own influence thereto. Thus, while Neptune is essentially unworldly, spiritual, a strong aspect of Mars thereto may cause it to show as worldly in the extreme, the spiritual influence of Neptune intensifying the desires of Mars. And so, of course, with the other planets.

The next consideration will be the Sun and the Moon.

which form on the whole the quickest and best index to the character by what has been called the "polarity."

The Sun is the constructor, or the individual centre, the motive point; and the place of the Sun at birth indicates the root, so to speak, out of which the real character springs, so that the sign in which it is found will mark off the chief characteristics of the INDIVIDUALITY, or *real internal person*.   The Moon, on the other hand, represents the coherer, the preserver, the focusing agency through which this internal power or mode of energy expresses itself, the exterior nature with all its petty limitations and restrictions and prejudices—in a word, the PERSONALITY. In accordance, therefore, with the position of the Moon, its sign and its aspects, together with the nature of the ascending sign and its ruler, and the position and aspects of the latter, so will the character be expressed: the importance of these influences being in the order given, the most powerful and enduring being the sign-position and aspects of the Moon.

To make this idea as clear as possible, let us think of the Sun, Moon, and Ascendant as *spirit*, *soul*, and *body* respectively.   The Sun, as the spirit, will require the Moon, as the soul, to express it, in addition to that which is permanent in the body through the Ascendant.   This idea is very interesting when we come to think of the law of heredity.   The body is given to us by our parents, symbolized by the tenth and fourth houses.   Upon this body are stamped the facial peculiarities and other general characteristics of the parents, and with them, in part, the family character   When a negative sign rises, the mother will give the greatest impression; when a positive, the father.

This body is constantly changing its molecules, and in

seven years, so scientists tell us, its whole make-up will have completely changed. Now, by the end of the first seven years the Ego, or soul, will have fully entered and controlled it, and will begin to impress its influence upon the body. Then, as life advances, the lunar influence will become gradually more and more prominent. It can now be easily understood how the environment will greatly influence those who continue to respond to the rising sign, and how great will be the importance of change of environment; for it will not be until this takes place that the lunar influence will have chief control, and the Personality, as represented by the Moon, becomes more and more marked and distinct. It is usually the Moon's important aspects which indicate these changes. Now from the polarization of the Moon to the Sun we learn the true nature of the Personality, and as there will be 144 of these different "polarities," we shall at once see that there are 144 totally different and distinct characters, *irrespective of the other planetary configurations.*

We will now consider these polarities, but it must be distinctly remembered that they are *general* only, for much will depend upon the part of the map in which the polarity falls, and the aspects to the Sun and Moon respectively; but in a general way the polarity will indicate the trend of the character. The SUN IN ARIES is in every respect intellectual, and produces reasoners and thinkers and independent characters, those who are born pioneers. They will be leaders, always aiming to be at the head of everybody and everything: and they will give in to none who cannot reason.

Now each "polarity" of the Sun in Aries and the

Moon in any of the other signs will accentuate or restrain this head nature as follows : *—

☉-♈ —☽-♈   Intense mental activity; great love of independence and self-reliance. (*Zola, Duke of Cambridge.*)

☉-♈ —☽-♉   Intellectual, strong - willed, stubborn; very determined and dogmatic. (*See Map No.* 7.)

☉-♈ —☽-♊   Mentally expressive, expansive, restless and changeable.

☉-♈ —☽-♋   Extremely sensitive, retentive in memory, and intuitive. (*General Booth.*)

☉-♈ —☽-♌   Ardent, affectionate, harmonious, philanthropic, and intuitive. (*Philippa Forest: see "Modern Astrology,"* October 1906.)

☉-♈ —☽-♍   Discriminative, persevering, critical, logical and scientific.

☉-♈ —☽-♎   Perceptive, sensitive and sensational.

☉-♈ —☽-♏   Combative and ardent, somewhat jealous and sensual. (*Grundy, the playwright.*)

☉-♈ —☽-♐   Active, extreme, hasty and restless.

☉-♈ —☽-♑   Exacting, thoughtful and receptive. (*Lord Milner.*)

☉-♈ —☽-♒   Studious, artistic and enterprising. (*See Map, No.* 3.)

☉-♈ —☽-♓   Executive, harmonious and logical. (*David Christie Murray.*)

* The names added are those of noteworthy persons who have these positions at birth ; it must not, of course, be inferred that the descriptions given will necessarily apply to them without any further qualification.

From this example * it will be seen that the blending of the polarities depends primarily upon the Sun's position, the Moon giving expression to the characteristics therein implied, but coloured by the nature of the sign it is in. For instance, take ☉-♈—☽-♑. Here we have an impulsive martial solar influence restrained by a restrictive saturnine lunar influence. This polarity will not work harmoniously; for the internal portion of such an individual will be larger than the external, and this will cause a continual war between the spirit and the mind, the latter seeking externals, while the spirit is striving to break down the conventional and limited Saturn, and this struggle would go on until one conquered—which in this case would be the Sun, fire (♈) being stronger than earth (♑).

We will briefly discuss a few of the polarities in order that these ideas may be clearly grasped.

The Sun in Taurus and the Moon in Virgo would be a good polarity, because the ☉ and ☽ are in signs of like nature, both being earthy; therefore this would give a good practical business character. Again, the Sun in Leo and Moon in Aries; here we see the mind or head seeking ever to express the feelings of the heart through poetry or philosophy.

If in considering these polarities we blend the triplicities, it will be very easy to judge of the nature of each as follows:— The *fiery* signs express the spiritual and philosophic; the *airy*, the mental, artistic, and refined; the *watery*, the emotional or sensuous nature; and the

---

* The various polarities of the Sun and Moon are given in brief in *Everybody's Astrology* (1s.), and in much greater detail in pp. 71–156 of *Astrology for All, Part I.* (7s. 6d.), obtainable from the publishers of this book.

earthy, the sensual, business, or scientific types of character. It will not be difficult to blend these polarities when the nature of each triplicity is understood. For instance, water will not blend well with fire, nor will air mix well with earth; but earth and water will make mud, as Eleanor Kirk says, or clay, or paint, or crystals, as the case may be. The whole secret of *character* is contained in these polarities, for if the Moon is unable to express the Sun, then there will not be that harmony in the character that will enable the disposition to be free and happy.

The ascending sign, and the sign or signs in which the majority of the planets are placed, will greatly influence character, from the standpoint of their inherent or primal nature, as follows :—

The *earthy* signs rule all that is physical, and of the material or earthy nature, showing that the chief experiences of the life are to be gained by material and physical objects; and it will be found that the interests of those who have many planets in such signs will lie in those pursuits and attractions that have connection with the solid or practical as the basis for all action. They will move slowly but surely, and their characters will be steady, patient, and enduring. Moving chiefly in the business world, they will come in contact with hard matter-of-fact experiences, and will persist in learning the lessons of life from appearances and at first-hand.

The *watery* signs are connected with all that is emotional, sensational, and romantic; it is the critical stage between the purely physical and the truly mental condition, and its dangers are therefore great to the unwary. The character of those who come under the

K

influence of the watery signs is liable to be greatly affected by others; they will be in danger of the hypnotic and psychological influence of those who can play upon their feelings and emotions. They will be what is termed psychics and mediums, and will be drawn more toward the emotional than the physical modes of life. Always impressionable, they will have what are called inspirations; frequently imaginative and fanciful, they will daydream and drift into all which affords experience through sensation and feeling. The stage and all that excites and moves the emotions will attract them, for it will afford the best medium whereby they can express their psychic, emotional nature.

The *airy* signs are intimately connected with the mind or mental condition, and the whole range of the mental vision is encompassed by the airy and human signs. Therefore those who are found with the indicators of character in these signs will incline toward the artistic and professional modes of life. Ever seeking mental culture and refinement, they will have in their character all that is free, independent, and humane. They will move in a sphere of usefulness and thoughtfulness, and have little or no desires toward the animal or sensual inclinations, but delight more in the sensuous and delicate ideas of existence. Mental pursuits and refined society will have a great influence upon the character of such.

The *fiery* signs have more to do with the spiritual and devotional side of life, and an earnest and eager aspiration after the higher and more truly real modes of life will shape the character more after an ideal type than any of the other signs. The ideal will be ever before them, and their danger will lie in the following of the ideal to the detriment of the practical. An innate religious sentiment will urge them to constantly try to live to the best of their whole nature, and all that is noble, sincere, and true will ever be a magnet to attract them away from the sordid and the mean.

These four divisions must be well considered in all their varied phases, but the root of each, or the basic quality, will be as follows:—

EARTHY.   Practical and material, commercial, intellectual and scientific.

WATERY.   Emotional and plastic, sympathetic and resolvent; reproductive.

AIRY.   Refined and artistic, given to abstract ideas.

FIERY.   Spiritual and idealistic, energizing and creative.

Three other divisions must, however, be considered in addition with the above, that is, the Cardinal or movable, Mutable or common, and Fixed. The *cardinal* will make the character acute, active, restless, aspiring and changeable. The *common* or mutable, indifferent, slow, vacillating and hesitating, yet tractable and impressionable. The *fixed* will make it determined, decisive, firm, ambitious and unbending, slow to move, yet irresistible when started.

We shall now illustrate the foregoing remarks by the following maps, taking persons well known to every student, so that they may examine their lives according to the rules we have given for judging character.

Napoleon III., Map No. 3, was born under Capricorn, an earthy and cardinal sign, a sign giving a melancholic, but ambitious, persistent, and political nature. The ruling planet is posited in the M.C. in the fixed and watery sign

Scorpio giving a reserved, tenacious, determined, and secretive character. The Sun is in the martial, fiery, and cardinal sign Aries, and in conjunction with Mars, giving

CONTRAST MAP, No. 3.

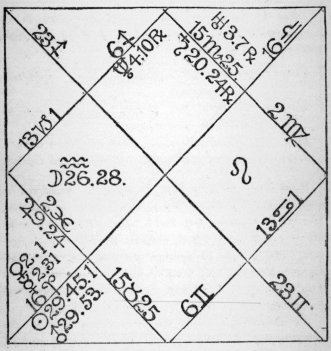

Capricorn rising, Saturn ruler in Scorpio.
⊙ in ♈. ☽ in ♒.

assertion and courage and all the impulse of a combatant, while the Moon is in the day-house of Saturn, the fixed and airy sign Aquarius, thus allowing the character to express itself through an ingenious intellectual and thoughtful medium. It will be seen that a clear and concise method of arriving at Napoleon III.'s character and disposition

CONTRAST MAP, No. 4.

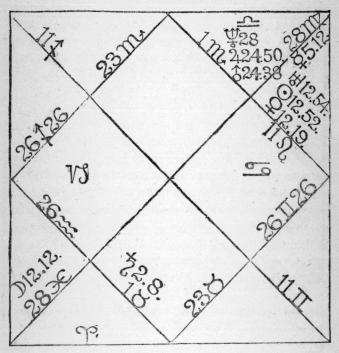

Sagittarius rising, Jupiter ruler in Libra.
☉ in ♌. ☽ in ♓.

may be arrived at in this way. His was a perfect blend of saturnine and martial influences. The saturnine side of his character was cold, hard, resistless, and calculating.

He could be cruel and unbending, the aspects tending in every way to strengthen the positions above noted.

Percy Bysshe Shelley, the poet, Map No. 4, taken from "Fate and Fortune," shows a wonderful contrast. Here we have the fiery and common sign Sagittarius ascending, with Jupiter, the ruler, in the humane sign Libra, and placed in the ninth house in conjunction with Mars and Neptune. This gave him at once the artistic and prodigal tendency and poetical enthusiasm. The Sun in Leo, in conjunction with Venus and Uranus, increased both the ideality and the mentality; while the Moon in Pisces gave the emotional tinge to his life, and conferred upon him his extreme sensitiveness and receptivity. With Shelley the Jupiterian influence predominated, with Napoleon the Martial-Saturnian—truly a contrast in character, and a subject well worthy of the student's careful study before proceeding.

In addition to the primary influence of the Ascendant, Ruling planet, Sun and Moon, all the planets play a more or less important part in the formation of the character. Each planet has a special quality of its own, which it imparts to the particular point which receives its influence. And if that point be the Ascendant, then the whole life is coloured with its quality and influence.

It will now be as well to particularize a few of the qualities over which the planets preside, dividing them into two sections for each, which we will for the present call the active and the passive. As will be seen, we have made the *active* represent the best side of the planets' natures, or that which they are intended to express; and the *passive* their reverse side, *i.e.* when not clearly expressed, owing to afflictions with other planets, uncongenial signs, unfavourable houses, &c.

SUN ACTIVE.*

Honourable, powerful, ambitious, noble, commanding, supreme, august, positive, lofty, sublime, radiant, determined, firm, dignified, effective, eminent, elevated, competent, faithful, distinguished, glorious, illustrious, loyal, staunch, true, absolute, potent.

SUN PASSIVE.

Authoritative, arbitrary, despotic, arrogant, proud, dictatorial, disdainful, haughty, domineering.

MOON ACTIVE.

Ambitious of fame, notoriety or excellence, adaptable, receptive, educative, practical, ready and expeditious, sympathetic, sensitive, refined, intuitive, careful, economical, acquisitive, tenacious.

MOON PASSIVE.

Frivolous, trifling, giddy, wanton, fickle, hysterical, petty, conceited, puerile, paltry, vain, idle, dreamy, nonsensical, passive, weak, lethargic, awkward, changeable, full of personal pride, insane or demented.

MERCURY ACTIVE.

Able, skilful, qualified, expert, successful, productive, vigilant, sensible, prudent, reasonable, observant, active, quick, energetic, alert, prompt, adroit, thoughtful, clever,

---

* The only way to give a good general notion of the idea to be conveyed, is by a string of adjectives expressive of some of the many characteristics manifested by those coming chiefly under the special influence noted. It will be seen that some of these are mutually exclusive, and this is inevitable, for in no one case will *all* the characteristics mentioned be exhibited, so that the list given is merely intended to convey a "general idea"—necessarily vague, but useful nevertheless.

smart, accomplished, intellectual, vivacious, expeditious, nimble, eloquent, fluent, ready, lucid, vivid, "mercurial."

MERCURY PASSIVE.

Shiftless, grovelling, mean, worthless, servile, base, despicable, artful, incompetent, desultory, rambling, fitful, intermittent, embarrassed, diffuse, discursive, digressive, fraudulent, imposing, knavish, thievish.

VENUS ACTIVE.

Loving, chaste, virtuous, affectionate, grateful, harmonious, pure, modest, cheerful, refined, innocent, idealistic, blissful, harmless, humane, graceful, pleasing, happy, amiable, charming, companionable, agreeable, docile, tender.

VENUS PASSIVE.

Soft, sensuous, approbative, disorderly, untidy, thoughtless, emotional, too fond of ease and pleasure, indolent, immodest, lewd.

MARS ACTIVE.

Bold, brave, courageous, plucky, gallant, hardy, robust, spirited, energetic, active, intrepid, adventurous, fearless, defensive, full of expedients, ingenious, venturesome, generous, zealous.

MARS PASSIVE.

Profligate, depraved, vicious, abusive, slanderous, violent, irritable, repellent, resentful, choleric, audacious, sensual, destructive, rash, envious, vulgar, coarse, rude, virulent, fierce, wild, savage, rough, impatient, impulsive, combative, contemptuous, disbelieving.

JUPITER ACTIVE.

Benevolent, philanthropic, beneficent, hopeful, generous, compassionate, merciful, sympathetic, liberal, free, truthful, frank, unsophisticated, unaffected, pure, moral, affable, jovial, honest, bountiful, munificent, sincere, charitable, pious, and devotional.

JUPITER PASSIVE.

Prodigal, thriftless, improvident, extravagant, lavish, dissipated, wasteful, pretentious, hypocritical.

SATURN ACTIVE.

Just, impartial, fair, accurate, definite, precise, exact, responsible, constant, contemplative, persistent, steady, pertinacious, stable, persevering, industrious, prompt, punctual, considerate, heedful, careful, arduous, assiduous, diligent, zealous, provident, enduring, serious, resolute, frugal, thrifty, acquisitive, earnest, calm, patient, deep, profound, reserved, reflective, grave, calculating, temperate.

The *airy* signs are those through which **Saturn-active** will find its best expression.

SATURN PASSIVE.

Gloomy, melancholic, morbid, doubtful, sceptical, fearful, slow, perverse, indifferent, unjust, callous, limited, incompetent, laborious, deceitful, imposing, impotent, obscure, covetous, procrastinating, timorous, despondent, sad, repining, heavy, morose, cold, sulky, avaricious, mercenary, exacting, dishonourable, despicable, infamous, hateful.

The signs through which the Saturn-passive finds its best expression are the *earthy*.

To these we may add :—

URANUS.

Bohemian, romantic, roving, eccentric, peculiar, intuitive, inspirational, creative, inventive, talented.

NEPTUNE.

Psychic, spiritualistic, uncommon, elusive, subtly attractive or repellent.

As explained before, a great deal depends upon the sheath, or sign, through which the planet is manifesting; also the aspects from the other planets. With regard to the former, the signs over which the planet is lord will express its nature best, the positive signs displaying more of the active nature, and the negative the passive, according to receptivity. Then we must consider the exaltations, for, next to when in their own signs, planets are strongest when exalted. So far as we know, no author seems to have correctly understood or interpreted the exaltations of the planets, and now that we have before us the quality of each planet, we may partly explain them.

The Sun, as already stated, is exalted in *Aries*, Jupiter in *Cancer*, Saturn in *Libra*, and Mars in *Capricorn*—the four cardinal signs. There is an esoteric meaning for this which is very wonderful, but which we cannot now go into, so we will examine the question merely from the exoteric or practical standpoint. It will be noted that each of these cardinal signs is the head of one of the trinities (see pp. 172, 173).

Aries is the head of the Intellectual Trinity, and was not the choice of Aries as the Sun's exaltation a wise and accurate one, for the intellect illuminates the man as a whole, and the Sun does likewise for the system of which it is the centre, its home being Leo. We should, therefore, look for the unity of head and heart from this grand exaltation. Let us then take Jupiter who is exalted in the head of the Maternal Trinity, and whose duty, it is clear, is to succour and sustain, to nourish and preserve. Could we think of any other planet better suited than Jupiter to lead the way of this trinity? We think not, and his exaltation in Cancer is beyond doubt a happy one. Next comes Saturn, and for his impartial, fair, reflective, and calculating nature we have the sign of the balances as his exaltation. Here it is that Justice holds the scales, and here, in the head of the Reproductive or Self-Conscious Trinity, the life elements are weighed and either wisely conserved and sent up to the brain for intellectual illumination and the expression of Saturn-active, or misused, thereby producing a distorted element of creative force. Lastly, Mars finds a happy exaltation in Capricorn, the head of the Serving trinity. "He who is the greatest amongst you let *him* be the servant of all," said the great Teacher. And who else could we find so active and courageous to serve as the warrior Mars? for in this he fulfils the commandment that the first shall be last, and the last first.

We have now reached a point where it is necessary to consider aspects, in their bearing upon the character. It is often very perplexing to the student to find two or more aspects in operation of totally different natures, it being difficult for him to understand which will be the strongest. Look at Map No. 3, Napoleon III. The Moon is in square aspect with Saturn and sextile Mars. It is therefore perceived that cold and heat are at one and the same time being poured into the Moon in the Ascendant. Here we have quick and impulsive energy coming from Mars (which gives audacity, boldness, courage, and adventurous enterprise) steadied by the Saturnian influx from the negative house of Mars, and with four planets in the houses of Mars it is not at all difficult to perceive that Mars has chief influence. Behind all the martial endowment, however, is the calculation, persistence, patience, and perseverance indicated by Saturn, added to which is the influence of the Moon from the positive house of Saturn.

A harmonious arrangement of the aspects may be made up from the active and passive qualities by blending them to express the influence by aspect of planets that are not of a sympathetic nature. Thus Mars, who is antipathetic to Saturn, will when in affliction therewith express the joint influence of both when passive. In the same way Mars, who is also antipathetic to Jupiter, will when in affliction therewith express Jupiter-passive; and so on with the other planets. A few of the aspects, for example, may be rendered as follows :—

[NOTE.—The Moon always expresses the passive side of a planet in affliction, and the active when well aspected.]

Mercury in Good Aspect with Saturn.

Discrimination, distinction, discernment, judgment, tact, carefulness, heed, vigilance, practicalness, reflectiveness, contemplativeness.

Mercury in Good Aspect with Jupiter.

Careful, steady, earnest, thoughtful, sympathetic, charitable, sincere, truly religious.

Mercury afflicted by Saturn.

Dishonest, fraudulent, perfidious, treacherous, cunning, rascally, unjust, exacting, false, unstable, critical, cynical, cowardly, poor-spirited.

Mercury afflicted by Jupiter.

Unreliable, hypocritical, deceitful, insincere.

Mercury in Good Aspect with Mars.

Fluent, speedy, rapid, expansive, fecund, brisk, operative, lively, agile, active, clear-sighted, eagle-eyed, deft, clever, industrious, romantic.

Mercury in Good Aspect with Venus.

Artistic, poetical, dramatic, of kind mind and gentle disposition.

Mercury afflicted by Mars.

A disputer, wrangler, exaggerator, unmethodical, disconnected, argumentative, impulsive, rash, untruthful, inquisitive, volatile, whimsical, fanciful, unreal, foolish, vain.

Jupiter in Good Aspect to Saturn.

Sympathetic, sincere, grateful, steady, profound, contemplative, meditative, just, and withal generous.

Jupiter afflicted by Saturn.

Credulous, hypocritical, deceitful, shabby.

Saturn afflicted by Mars.

Degraded, selfish, malevolent, misanthropic, cruel, austere, unrelenting, obdurate, ill-natured, churlish, penurious, miserly, niggardly, servile, debased, greedy.

Jupiter in Good Aspect to Mars.

Generous, extravagant, lavish, stimulative, enthusiastic.

Jupiter afflicted by Mars.

Prodigal, foolishly generous, wasteful, riotous, dissipated, thoughtless.

Mars in Good Aspect to Venus.

Affectionate, sensuous, strong emotions and feelings, prone to love at first sight.

Mars afflicted by Venus.

Passionate, sensual, fond of pleasure, improvident, dissipated, careless, emotional, untidy.

Mars in Good Aspect to Uranus.

Very energetic, extremely active and self-reliant, quick, original, enthusiastic, ambitious.

Mars afflicted by Uranus.

Restless, excitable, impulsive, rash, nervous, irritable, fidgety.

Venus in Good Aspect to Uranus.

Romantic, original, talented, sublime, wonderfully artistic, musical, fond of the mystical.

Venus afflicted by Uranus.

Sensationally romantic, morbid in love affairs, foolish in sex matters, melodramatic, subject to uncommon experiences with the opposite sex.

Mercury in Good Aspect to Uranus.

Original, metaphysical, astrological, profound in thought, and deep in argument; brilliant and wise.

Mercury afflicted by Uranus.

Critical, sarcastic, "cranky," peculiar, uncommon, antiquated, nervous, mysterious.

CHAPTER XVII

THE MENTAL QUALITIES

BEFORE we form any definite or decided conclusions with regard to character we must fully consider the Mind, through which the Soul, as the cream of character, so to speak, can manifest.

Character is Destiny. And the mind is the pilot of that destiny.

The vast majority of students of Astrology, in common with those who as yet have not undertaken the task of self-knowledge, have not yet realized that the mind is not the man, neither have they distinguished the difference between the real and permanent character, and the mind. To simplify the difference between the two we shall consider The Mind as quite distinct from the Permanent Character (or, as it is called by occult students, the *Ego*).

It has been generally understood that Mercury is the chief ruler of the mind: in a measure this is quite correct, but all the planets play a very important part in its formation. The chief mental rulers are the Moon, Saturn, and Mercury; which three, through their final expression in Jupiter, hand up, as *memory*, the cream of the life experiences to the benefic planet Venus, there to remain as *permanent character*.

We may now distinguish between Mind and Character by classing the former under the Lunar scale, and the latter under the Solar, as shown in the accompanying diagram :—

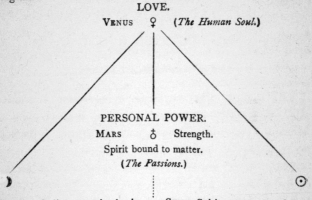

LOVE.

VENUS   ♀   (*The Human Soul.*)

PERSONAL POWER.

MARS   ♂   Strength.

Spirit bound to matter.

(*The Passions.*)

MOON. — Ordinary animal instincts, unconditioned consciousness.

ħ SATURN. — Crystallized or limited material consciousness.

(*The lower or brain mind.*)

SUN.—Spirit essence, or the uncoloured Individuality, unconditioned.

♃ JUPITER. — Spirit coloured, conditioned, or Individualized.

(*The higher consciousness.*)

WISDOM.

MERCURY   ☿   The Mind.

Human, Physical, Consciousness.

(*The Thinker.*)

This diagram will now give us a clue to the workings of the mental qualities. It will indicate the chief factors as the Moon and Mercury. The former is the medium through which the senses are excited into action, and may be considered as the blind or un-self-conscious, animal part of our nature.

L

First the MOON is what we may term the animal or instinctive consciousness; it is blind in its operations, and must be aspected by the planets to give it colour and definiteness. It may be thought of as the lowest expression of mind, receptive to contact from without, but not from within. Fluidic in nature, it is coloured and impressed by environment. This mind, as instinct, is common to all animals, and it is therefore merely tantamount to *physical consciousness*.

Now, passing from the Moon to SATURN, we obtain a more crystallized or concrete condition of this mind-stuff, or instinct; and when represented by Saturn, it becomes the personal or limited mind, the self-conscious understanding, the " I am I." This is the king of the lower self, or the reaper of the suffering and sorrows of the personal life. It is the *lower mind*, that lingers in its journey through the halls of intellect and narrow conventionalities, its desires being of the earth, earthy.

From Saturn we pass upward to MERCURY, the ruler of the mind when freed from its limitations, the bondage of self-seeking, love, fame, and personal ambitions. It then becomes mind, distinct from the animal, and marked by purely humane tendencies. It now reasons upon its past experiences and passes into the intellectual stages. Looking deeper into these joint factors of the mind, we may think of Saturn as the objective perception, the practical, matter-of-fact, and orthodox or stereotyped intellect; mind in every sense of the word objective, having its highest attainments in science. Mercury as reflective, the thinker, or reasoner Always mutable, it has in itself the combined qualities of positive and negative, or male and female, and is therefore sexless, or rather, hermaphrodite. It is impressed and influenced by the planets with which it has the nearest aspect, colouring and tingeing the mind in accordance with their nature. This planet, therefore, is the first that we must consider in all matters connected with the *mind proper*.

Our senses are quick, or slow, in accordance with the position and aspects of the MOON. Each of the five senses has a ruler, and each is well developed or merely latent in accordance with the planet's strength or weakness; but the whole of them are collected and manifested by the Moon, which represents the *Animal Soul*. It is dependent upon contact from without for the sensation or physical representation. But when turned inward, and exalted to a condition that is not dependent upon contact from without, being translated into direct consciousness or spiritual perception, these same "senses," or vehicles of perception, are in their totality represented by the Sun.

There is a critical stage between these two conditions which is called the human soul, represented by Venus. This planet presides over the feelings and emotions, its lowest limit being physical contact or *touch*, from which point it recedes inward until the highest condition, Soul-feeling, is realized. Of the other senses, Mercury governs *sight*, Saturn *hearing*, Jupiter *smelling*, and Mars *taste*.

Passing from the senses, we come to the rational, intellectual, and reasoning condition of the mind, which is ruled by MERCURY. The dual nature of this planet, which comes from its convertible nature, enables it to translate the whole of its impressions into either the practical or the ideal. The whole of its impressions thus affect Body, Soul, and Spirit, and its precise workings upon either one or the whole of these factors may be known from the nature of the planets with which Mercury is in aspect.

We must not forget that the Moon is unconditioned consciousness, as common to the animal and therefore purely instinctive, while Mercury is human consciousness, which results from thinking and reasoning, and should always be thought of as The Thinker. It will be easily seen how the Moon will act when in any of the different signs, or when in aspect to any of the planets which preside over the particular senses. The Moon gives the mind its start, in fact, each atom and molecule of the human organism obtaining a self-conscious condition before it can translate its experiences into the brain cells, where the impressions are stored as memory. All experience, therefore, first comes by way of the Moon, which is the shuttle that weaves the fabric upon the loom of the Individual's manifestation. Its pattern is the choice of the desires of the Soul, who wears the garment of many-coloured threads.

The position of the Moon at birth must decide the future condition, or fate, during the one earth-life of the ordinary man. Without laying down any arbitrary rule we may observe that, should the Moon be increasing in light at birth,* the full nature of the sign it is in will be expressed throughout the life; but should it be decreasing in light,† we may expect the opposite to be evolved. For instance, if the Moon (decreasing) be in Aries, from an impulsive condition the native will advance to the balance of Libra, and so on.

The senses will always be hot and easily excited when

* *i.e.* passing from the ☌ ☉ toward the ☍ ☉.
† *i.e.* passing from the ☍ ☉ toward the ☌ ☉.

the Moon is in the martial and fiery signs, but cold when in the saturnine and earthy signs. Each sign will colour and impress the Moon with its nature, and each aspect will tinge the "sensitive plate" of the lunar orb, according to the nature of the aspecting planet. This applies also to Mercury with regard to the mind. If the mind and senses, Mercury and the Moon, are linked together and afflicted, then there results a tendency toward abuse of powers and faculties.

In a previous chapter we gave the conditions of Mercury when active and passive. The active state is that in which the THINKER is active and of the positive, seeking type. But when passive, the thoughts are latent, and the mind, owing to its lethargic condition, can be easily acted upon by adverse currents from other minds. For this reason a mind that will not act for itself cannot obtain real knowledge, but must always be dependent upon others for information, and so in time is bound to lapse into a retrograde condition, finally falling into the senses to again re-awaken through painful experiences.

Mars quickens the action of Mercury, while Saturn retards and steadies the mental expression. Both these conditions belong to the material or practical side of expression, whereas Jupiter and Venus elevate into the idealistic state. To give every shade and colour to the mind, the swift Mercury, who is the "Winged Messenger of the Gods," forms many kaleidoscopic mental pictures during his cycle.

But there is a mental ruler that we have not as yet mentioned, and were it not for the fact that all earnest students of Astrology come directly under the influence of this planet, we could afford to dispense with the mention ot its name, let alone a description of its influence. This planet is the mystic URANUS, ⛢, the mental ruler who takes in hand those who have worked through the Mercurial conditions. This planet promises to those who rise above the mental conditions offered by Mercury, a state of mind that transcends the ordinary reasoning to a height as far in comparison as that between Mercury and the Moon. It governs the sixth sense, which may be considered as including all the others in one, and which is called INTUITION. It is direct and inward perception. As apart from the thinker it may be called the Knower, and its full interpretation can be known only by those who come under this influence. Original to a degree, it cannot be impressed by physical objects, but needs a metaphysical state in which to find its expression. It is allied to "fourth dimensional space." The period of this planet is rapidly approaching, and about the year 1914 the dawn of its manifestation will appear. Then the consciousness of those who have refused to leave the objects of sense and intellect of the conventional order, will be rudely shaken by the rapidly spreading knowledge of the deeper mysteries.

Before proceeding to illustrate the mental qualities by contrast maps we would advise the students to re-read, and be sure that they understand, what has previously been said about (1) the Twelve Houses, (2) the Twelve Signs, and (3) the nature of each Planet and Aspect with regard to the *mind*, so that they may readily comprehend what follows.

CHAPTER XVIII

MIND AND CHARACTER CONTRASTED

IT will now be necessary to contrast mind and character, so that an accurate judgment of the distinct value of each may be formed. The septenary division of man's principles, as defined by the ancient Chaldears, and now interpreted through the Wisdom Religion, will aid us considerably in our understanding of what Man in reality consists.

The principles in each of us are *identical*, but their arrangement is so different that it becomes absolutely necessary for us to thoroughly understand these principles before we can have any conception of how extremely complex our natures are; and this we must know ere we can proceed to study them, as shown by the distribution of the planets representing these principles in the various parts of the heavens at birth.

According to this division we have seven principles, and six vehicles, or bodies, the highest principle being *outside* of all manifestation—the real man himself, or the *Atma*. This atma clothes itself first in a spiritual body, and then again in what is called the soul body; these three making the triad, the Three-in-One. This tri-unity then becomes sheathed in (4) a lower *mind-body*, (5) in the *astral body* of passions and desires, called the animal soul, and (6) finally in the etheric double, which is the counterpart of

(7) the physical body, the whole being immersed in matter through this physical body; thus is spirit seven times veiled.

It can thus be seen how character must become destiny, for we are certainly destined according to the condition of the bodies in which we are clothed, and we are building them through that character daily, (consciously or unconsciously), this being entirely the work of the Spirit. Let us see how.

In the last diagram we gave spirit as Unconditioned Individuality, represented by the Sun. It is unconditioned,

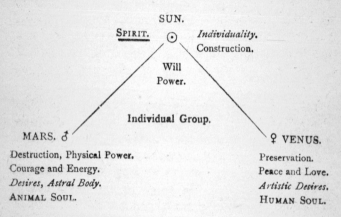

SUN.

SPIRIT. ⊙ *Individuality.*
Construction.

Will
Power.

Individual Group.

MARS. ♂ ♀ VENUS.

Destruction, Physical Power. Preservation.
Courage and Energy. Peace and Love.
Desires, Astral Body. *Artistic Desires.*
ANIMAL SOUL. HUMAN SOUL.

pure in essence, and free (within certain limits), in accordance with the nature of the body through which it is working, and the density of the matter with which it has surrounded itself. It may always be defined as the WILL, and is moved, when linked to matter, solely by *desire*, until at last it rises superior to desire, and is moved by deliberate choice or *intention*. It can be seen that the will as represented by the Sun will be the chief factor in the formation of character.

Those symbols having the circle as component parts will,

therefore, be the character indicators. There is no simpler method of understanding both symbols and principles than the ordinary system adopted by the Christians of separating man into *body*, *soul*, and *spirit*. Under the head of the latter we may place the three planets Sun, Venus, and Mars, as shown in the diagram on the opposite page.

This first diagram will give some idea of the character and true mental rulers, the whole of which now have their best expression through Mercury; but those who advance

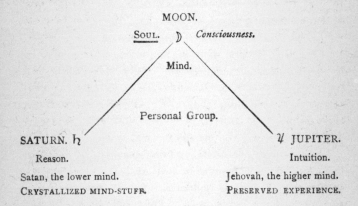

MOON.

SOUL. ☽ *Consciousness.*

Mind.

Personal Group.

SATURN. ♄   ♃ JUPITER.

Reason.   Intuition.

Satan, the lower mind.   Jehovah, the higher mind.
CRYSTALLIZED MIND-STUFF. PRESERVED EXPERIENCE.

beyond the present race will sound a higher octave in the planet Uranus, whose real symbol (⚇) is very significant.

Then we find the Soul represented by the Moon, Saturn, and Jupiter, as shown in the above diagram.

The whole of which is synthesized in the human consciousness so as also to find its final physical expression through Mercury.

The principal factor with regard to character, it will be seen, is the SUN, as the individual centre. When plunged into the lowest depths of the physical body, or matter, it is represented by the cross above the circle, as Mars—Spirit blind, or held captive. Then the struggle upward of the Spirit will offer every opportunity for the character to grow strong; growth in experience by exercise of its power, strength achieved by struggling against resistance. Thus courage and energy will be the distinguishing marks of the martial nature. In the old days such were the warriors who fought for and against law and order, often destroying only to rebuild. We can have many and various grades of the martial character, but at the root of all its manifestations we shall find destruction ever at work. He is the pioneer clearing the way for reconstruction, and without him in the world, there would be no pluck, energy, or enterprise. It is a necessary evil that we should destroy to construct. The Sun is construction, Mars is destruction. We can trace the workings of Mars in every nation. The old must ever be pulled down to make way for the new.

Let us examine the details of the character as indicated by Mars. We will consider it first when the mind has not entered into activity to guide it. It will then be known as impulse, force and violence. Blind and ignorant, it will be ever throwing itself against matter to realize itself; it will contest, rage, destroy; in every way it is the polar opposite to spirit when free from matter, being as it were adulterated by its contact with matter. Body after body and vehicle after vehicle, it will smash up and destroy, before it obtains control over it. Senses will be built up time after time, only to be destroyed again and again until each successive struggle ends in a more subjugated condition of the matter ensouled. But with each struggle it produces a vaporous mist which may be called the consciousness of its own creation; the result of its own experience. In this way does character work through lust to purity, from war to peace, till Mars finally gives way to Venus, in which symbol we find Spirit has worked its way through matter and surmounted the cross, ♀.

We can thus form some idea of how character is built up. When the will which has taken ages to conquer matter links itself with Mars, then is strength added; the courageous and fearless spirit has procured power, and we have everything that we can call physical strength. But when with Venus, we find strength balanced by tenderness, giving birth to that considerateness which we admire so much in the perfect gentle-man, who though strong is also *gentle*.

The twelve signs of the zodiac must now play their important part, for through them the principles obtain their colour and mode of expression, and in them is depicted the pilgrimage of the Ego. We may consider these twelve signs as existing for the purpose of manifestation with regard to the principles, just as our physical body exists for the manifestation of our spirit; and as we have seen that we have other bodies beside the physical, so we may find their counterparts in the zodiac. As explained in the first part of this work, there are four principal divisions of the signs, those that are concerned with physical evolution: physical—*earthy* ; emotional—*watery* ; mental—*airy* ; and spiritual—*fiery*. Then by another blending, we have the three great divisions of *cardinal*, *fixed*, and *mutable*, concerned with the spiritual side of evolution, and which represent the three primary qualities giving life its opportunities, as construction, preservation, and destruction, or as the Eastern sages term it, Rajas, Tamas, and Sattva, which may be said to mean activity, indifference, and peace. It is through these conditions that the transmutation of the baser metals into gold is performed, as also the moulding of character from gross to fine. If we now classify these twelve signs we shall have an index of ideas for character and mind building:—

OUT-GOING CYCLE (*Involution*).

♈︎ *Day house of* ♂	CARDINAL. Impulsive Indifferent Unfeeling	FIERY. Spiritual Idealistic Logical	INTELLECTUAL. Mental Pioneering Scientific
♉︎ *Night house of* ♀	FIXED. Cautious Steady Determined	EARTHY. Physical Stubborn Sensuous	INTELLECTUAL. Instinctive Plodding Material
♊︎ *Day house of* ☿	COMMON. Restless Volatile Humane	AIRY. Dualistic Ideal Artistic	INTELLECTUAL. Educational Executive Inventive

Intellectual Trinity.

♋︎ *House of the* ☽	CARDINAL. Sensitive Romantic Changeable	WATERY. Emotional Imaginative Fluidic	MATERNAL. Reflective Formative Nursing
♌︎ *House of the* ☉	FIXED. Determined Ambitious Constructive	FIERY. Spiritual Self-controlling Independent	MATERNAL. Emotional Protecting Persevering
♍︎ *Night house of* ☿	COMMON. Aspirational Retiring Hygienic	EARTHY. Sympathetic Practical Materialistic	MATERNAL. Discriminative Chaste Harmonious

Maternal Trinity.

The First House in the nativity, which is called the Ascendant, the cusp being that point which ascends on the eastern horizon at birth, is always the first and primary physical expression of character, the Ruler of the Sign thereon indicating the major part of the combined influences at work previous to birth. It is, as it were, the centralizing point into which all the principles are focused, and like the dot in the centre of the circle it is the root of all that is to be expressed. We gave some idea of this

RETURNING CYCLE (*Evolution*).

♎︎ *Day* *house or* ♀	CARDINAL. Equalizing Perceptive Imitative	AIRY. Socialistic Idealistic Intuitive	REPRODUCTIVE. Compassionate Affectionate Poetical	*Reproductive Trinity.*
♏︎ *Night* *house of* ♂	FIXED. Aggressive Distinctive Selfish	WATERY. Passional Subtle Mystical	REPRODUCTIVE. Sensual Reserved Conventional	
♐︎ *Day* *house of* ♃	COMMON. Impressionable Extreme Complex	FIERY. Ambitious Ardent Spiritual	REPRODUCTIVE. Demonstrative Prophetic Intuitive	
♑︎ *Night* *house of* ♄	CARDINAL. Sensitive Proud Political	EARTHY. Thoughtful Ambitious Cautious	SERVING. Utilitarian Organizing Persistent	*Serving Trinity*
♒︎ *Day* *house of* ♄	FIXED. Ingenious Faithful Just	AIRY. Scientific Experimental Intuitive	SERVING. Original Psychic Metaphysical	
♓︎ *Night* *house of* ♃	COMMON. Imitative Honest Timid	WATERY. Mediumistic Emotional Romantic	SERVING. Social Patient Silent	

when speaking of iron, the metal that Mars represents. As we there remarked, crude iron (♂, ♈︎) must be converted and tempered into fine steel (♑︎), and when this is complete we shall have made our own environment, an environment that responds to the dictates of our will; and from steel ($\hbar$) we shall then pass on to gold ($\odot$).

Every soul in manifestation has risen to that point at which he should express the character he has made for himself. Every manifestation, from the Logos downward, (and upward), has a particular and peculiar colour of its own. The rose and the violet are manifestations of the *same* spirit-essence, though their colour and scent differ. The planetary spirits are identical in essence, but each manifests a distinct feature of its own; and no matter how faint the manifestation in any human being may be, they are in essence of the same spirit, yet coloured differently Therefore, *there can be no equality*, in the physical and mental sense of the word, *each man being a law unto himself*. Realize this, and Astrology will open up a new field of practical good for this is its religious aspect blended with the scientific.

We have given in part the nature of the signs, and now we must judge of the essence poured into the sheaths, so as to know how the character will manifest. The will or spirit, $\odot$, will be strongest and most active in the Fixed signs, the central point of each trinity, the nature of the signs indicating the planes upon which it will act, *e.g.* Taurus, the practical and physical; Leo, the spiritual and idealistic; Scorpio, the emotional and passional; Aquarius, the refined and mental. Next in order will come the *Fiery* signs, Aries and Sagittarius; then the *Airy*, Gemini and Libra; next the *Earthy*, Virgo and Capricorn; and finally those in which the Sun is weakest, Cancer and Pisces, the *Watery*. The nature and disposition of the will and character may thus be judged from the position of the Sun. Mars will give force and tone to the character in the same way, while Venus will give refinement and finish in accordance with the sign she is in. Mars will prefer the *fiery* and *earthy* signs, while Venus will delight in the *watery* and *airy*.

The faces and decanates, as given in Chapter XIV., pp. 112–123, should be well studied, so that the character rulers may be fitted to them quickly. The characteristics of each part of the sign are given, and for general purposes they will be found fairly accurate. At any rate they may always be used with regard to the rising sign, which will, however, be modified by the planets that may fall in that particular degree of course. The faces holding the Sun, Venus, and Mars will, to a great extent, give the clue to the internal working of the character. Reference to Map 3 (p. 148) may help us to better understand this. Here Sun and Mars are in the third decanate of Aries, which we find is the negative portion, ruled by Jupiter, a fortunate prospect for the strong will and desires of Sun conjunction Mars. Venus, we find, mixes her influence with Mercury in the positive martial face of Aries, while the Ascendant is described by a positive saturnine Venus, the whole of which, both in description and characteristic, admirably fits the man of destiny.

The next point to consider, will be the planetary aspects to the character rulers; and here the mental qualities will blend themselves with the character, as "disposition." We have made it quite clear that the mind is not the real being, and there should now be no confusion between mind and character; yet both are dependent upon each other, for the character must have a mind to serve and express it.

To exemplify this still further, we will take the three

first signs of the zodiac, Aries, Taurus, and Gemini, the rulers of which are Mars, Venus, and Mercury. Having regard to what we have said of Spirit when working through matter, it can be seen why Mars leads in the order of the signs, but now note the exaltation of the planets, Sun in Aries, Moon in Taurus, and Mercury in Gemini.* Here we have spirit, soul, and body. When the principles have risen to the sheaths through which they can best manifest, this will be the order.

It will be seen that the Sun is friendly to Mars, the Moon to Venus, while Mercury is independent. Now refer to what we have said about positive and negative, and we shall have some clear ideas as to the nature of aspects. On the principle that likes harmonize and opposites disagree, we can gauge fairly well what the various aspects are likely to produce.

The cardinal signs are in square aspect to each other, and consist of positive and negative. For example, Aries and Libra are positive, and Cancer and Capricorn negative; Aries hot and fiery, Cancer cold and moist. Therefore we can understand that Moon square Mars would be a very evil aspect, out of which, owing to its conflicting nature, dire results might be expected It would be like plunging a red-hot piece of iron into cold water; the water might not boil, but a mass of vapour and mist would be the result.

Taking another view of the cardinal signs, we see how Mars square Saturn would act, positive in conflict with negative, the result depending upon the signs in which they were posited. If Mars fell in a negative sign and

---

* NOTE.—Mercury is stated by some to be exalted in Virgo, but it seems hardly reasonable that an inherently mental planet like Mercury should be exalted in an earthy sign. See note on p. 88.

Saturn in a positive, then the affliction would not be so severe, but more subdued and subtle. The Sun, Mars, and Jupiter are positive electric planets, while the Moon, Venus, and Saturn are negative and magnetic, Mercury being convertible. From this it will be seen that Sun square Saturn must be a greater evil than Sun square Mars, and that Moon square Mars is more evil than Moon square Saturn. There can be, however, no hard-and-fast rule as to the definite and exact working of the various aspects, and all text-books giving such should be avoided for that reason. In reading a map everything depends upon the *judgment*, and to assist this we now propose examining a few contrast maps, in which we shall judge both mind and character.

Before we do this, however, there is an important matter with regard to the mystic planet Uranus that should be stated. We have tried to give a reason for the nature of the various planets, but no definite and correct interpretation of Uranus has ever yet been given, and for this reason, that there are few who to-day come under the influence of this very wonderful planet. He governs a part of us that, if it is not the highest, is certainly the most important, and that is the Higher Self, as it is called. For it represents in totality the Sun, Venus, and Mercury, or the Spirit, Soul, and Body. It is the planet under which adepts and advanced occultists chiefly come, and it may be considered the synthesizing point of spirit, just as Mercury is of the mind. It is the planet that is to represent perfected humanity. At present he is "the houseless wanderer," and no sign has yet been accorded to him; but we shall deal with this planet in our judgments, which we shall now commence, beginning with the maps of two persons well known to many astrological students.

M

CONTRAST MAP, No. 5.

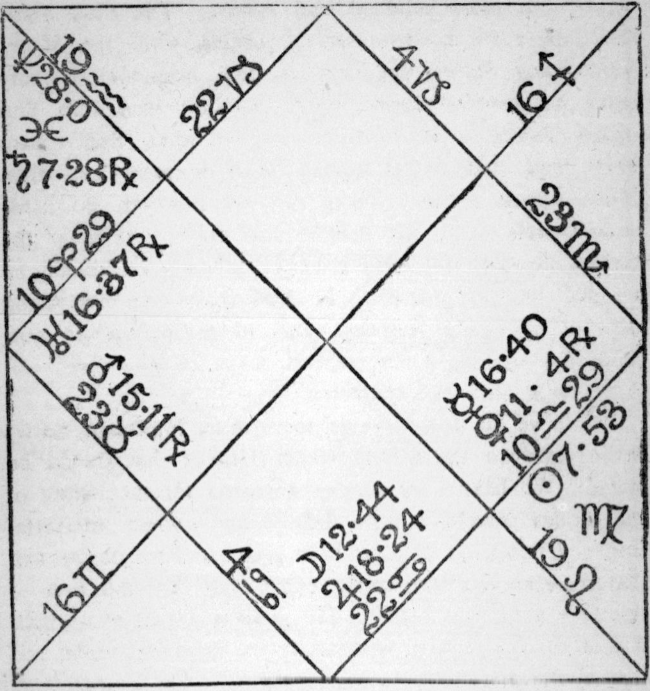

ASPECTS.

☉	□ ☽ : ☌ ♀	☽	☌ ♃ : ✶ ♂ : □ ♀ : □ ♅
♀	☌ ☿ : ☌ ☉ : □ ☽	♂	✶ ☽ : ✶ ♃
♃	☌ ☽ : ✶ ♂ : □ ☿	♄	△ ☽
♅	☍ ☿ : ☍ ♀ : □ ♃ : □ ☽	☿	☌ ♀ : ☍ ♅ : □ ♃

DECLINATIONS.

☉	3 S	♃	22 N
☽	17 N	♄	11 S
☿	6 S	♅	6 N
♀	12 S	♆	13 S
♂	14 N		

CONTRAST MAP, No. 6.

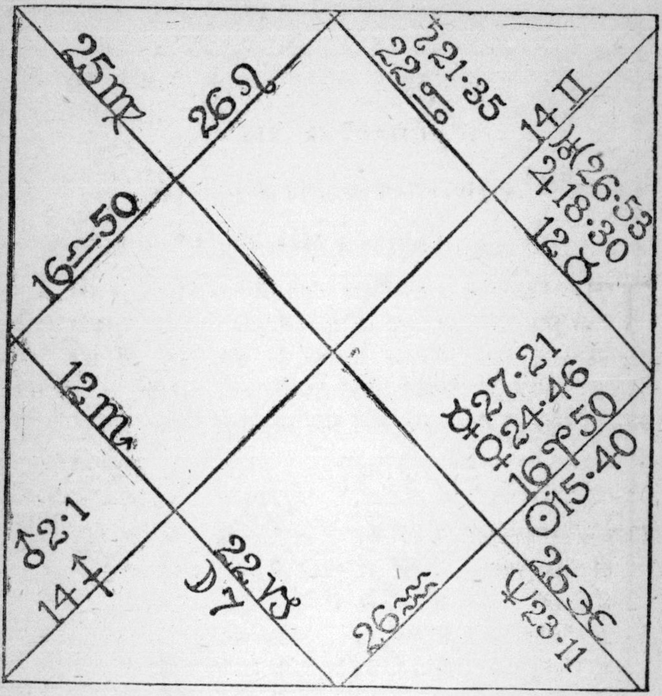
25♍
26♌
22♋
♄ 21·35
14♊
♅ 26·53
♃ 18·30
12♉
☿ 27·21
♀ 24·46
16♈50
☉ 15·40
25♓
♆ 23·11
26♒
22♑
☽ 7
♂ 2·1
14♐
12♏
16♎50

ASPECTS.

☉	□ ♄	☽	⚺ ♂
♀	□ ♄	♂	□ ☉ : P. ♅
♃	✱ ♄	♄	✱ ♃
♅	✱ ♄ : P. ♂	☿	☌ ♀ : □ ♄

DECLINATIONS.

☉	7 N	♃	17 N
☽	28 S	♄	22 N
☿	11 N	♅	19 N
♀	9 N	♆	4 S
♂	20 S		

CHAPTER XIX

DELINEATION OF TWO HOROSCOPES

(a) Contrast Map, No. 5 *

THE Cardinal and Fiery sign Aries, which is the first in the zodiac, rises in the Eastern horizon, the 10th degree and 29th minute being on the cusp of the first house, which is called the Ascendant. This is in the second (Solar) decanate and the negative face.

			Sign ruler.	Decanate ruler.	Face.
Cusp of Ascendant		♈ 10° 29′	♂ +	☉ +	−
♅	1st house	♈ 16° 37′	♂ +	☉ +	+
♂	1st „	♉ 15° 11′ ℞	♀ −	☿ −	−
☽	4th „	♋ 12° 44′	☽ −	♂ −	+
♃	4th „	♋ 18° 24′	☽ −	♂ −	−
☉	6th „	♎ 7° 53′	♀ +	♀ +	−
♀	7th „	♎ 11° 4′ ℞	♀ +	♄ +	−
☿	7th „	♎ 16° 40′	♀ +	♄ +	+
♄	12th „	♓ 7° 28′ ℞	♃ −	♃ −	+
♇	12th „	♒ 28° 0′	♄ +	♀ +	−

Mars, who is the ruler of the horoscope, is "accidentally" dignified, *i.e.* by position, being in the first house, corresponding to *Aries*. This planet is placed in the sign

---

* For the sake of those who may recognize this person, we may say that this map is calculated from the data furnished in the *Autobiography*.

Taurus 15° 11', the decanate ruled by Mercury. The Moon
and Jupiter are in the second decanate of Cancer, ruled
by Mars. The Sun is in the first decanate of Libra, ruled
by Venus, and Venus and Mercury are in the next portion,
ruled by Saturn, while Saturn falls in the first decanate of
Pisces, ruled by Jupiter. Returning now to the first house,
we find Uranus 6 degrees past the cusp of the Ascendant
and in the second decanate of Aries, ruled by the Sun
The whole may be summarized as on opposite page.

Four planets are in the houses of Venus, two in the
house of the Moon, one in the house of Jupiter, one in
that of Mars, and one in that of Saturn. Five are in positive signs, and four in negative. Five of the "decanates"
are positive and four negative, the reverse being true of the
"faces." Six planets are in Cardinal signs, two in Fixed,
and one in Common; and Cardinal signs are upon the
angles.

Having thus taken out the various factors in the horoscope, we tabulate the strength of the planets as follows :—

(1)	(2)	(3)	(4)
6 Cardinal.	1 Fire.	2 Fully Positive + + +.	6 Angular.
2 Fixed.	1 Earth.	2 ,, Negative – – –.	0 Succedent.
1 Common.	4 Air.	3 Semi-Positive + + –.	3 Cadent.
1 Exalted.	3 Water.	2 Semi-Negative – – +.	4 Oriental.*

This is the first key to the strength of the Map.

The *cardinal* signs indicate Activity, the *fixed* Feeling,
and the *common* Intellect. In their physical expression,
when manifested upon the external plane, they mean Fame,
Stability, and Mentality. Therefore, to interpret Column (1)

---

* *i.e.* RISING, or on the eastern or *oriental* portion of the map (left-
hand side). Planets SETTING, or on the western or right-hand portion of
the map, are said to be *occidental.*

in Map No. 5, we find every indication of Fame and Power, especially as it is borne out by Column (4), which must always be taken into consideration with Column (1); for many planets in cardinal signs but cadent houses will give merely desire for fame, with no ability or opportunity to achieve it.

The subject of this horoscope is one of the most famous and powerful women in Europe, having influenced the thought of thousands. Her eloquence is remarkable; indeed, she is one of the finest orators England has ever produced. Her sphere of influence extends wherever the English language is spoken, and even beyond. This extra-ordinary renown is indicated by the planets Venus and Mercury in the seventh, the house of the public; also by Moon conjunction Jupiter in Cancer, the sign of fame.

Passing to the next column, we find one planet in a fiery sign, which we interpret as the spiritual, one in the earthy or physical, three in the airy or mental, and three in the watery or emotional. The temperament, therefore, we judge as the mental-emotional. With regard to the positive and negative, we find balance; but as the major portion of the planets are in the electric portion of the map, the part of the heavens in which the signs rise and set, we judge more positive than negative.

In taking a general view of the map we find the first sign of the zodiac, Aries, ascending. Reference to the square map in Chapter XV. informs us that the First House rules the *life*, *health*, *personality*, *general appearance*, *character*, and *disposition*. Now taking the life and health, we find the ruling planet Mars in the fixed and physical sign Taurus, in sextile aspect with the Moon and Jupiter, and entirely free from affliction. This promises a sturdy build and muscular physique, a robust constitution, and a long and healthy life. The personality is in every way a strong one, firm and commanding yet subtle and persuasive.

The next consideration—most important of all—is the character and disposition. The characteristics for the third face of Aries, as given in Chapter XIV., read:—"serious and grave, intellectual and thoughtful; often good speakers." This is perfectly accurate in every detail. The physical description does not apply so closely, for the position of the ruler ♂, in ♉, tends to a firmer and less wiry build.

The sign Aries, as described in Chapter XVI., gives a frank, outspoken, combative, generous, assertive, impulsive, and intuitive nature; one fond of reason and argument. Being a fiery sign, moreover, it gives a spiritual and idealistic personality.

Mars, the ruling planet, being angular and in good aspect to the Moon and Jupiter, may be considered active. This in the same chapter under Mars-active describes the personality as bold, brave, courageous, plucky, gallant, hardy, robust, spirited, energetic, active, intrepid, fearless, adventurous, defensive, zealous, ingenious, venturesome, and generous. Taking also into consideration the planet Uranus in the Ascendant as the planet which stamps its mark upon the personality, we find the native inventive, creative, inspirational, intuitive, and talented. Thus we have a splendid personality, fearless, energetic, and generous. Not only may we predict that the iron of Mars may be turned into fine steel, but, as promised by the solar decanate ascending, into fine gold, the metal of the Sun.

We next come to the internal part of the nature, ruled by Sun, Venus, and Mars, the rulers of the "life" side, the highest expression of which is in character.

Here we find Mars expressing itself upon the physical plane through Taurus, the sign of the throat, through which organ our subject uses the major portion of her energy, having, as before stated, a wonderful gift of oratory. There is no affliction to this planet; and Jupiter, from the emotional sign Cancer, pours his influence of the highest consciousness into the ruler of the Personality, also the physical character indicator: (♃ ✶ ♂). Any aspect of Jupiter to Mars will be found to give an enthusiastic temperament, and a well directed enthusiasm may be said to be the leading characteristic of the subject of our delineation.

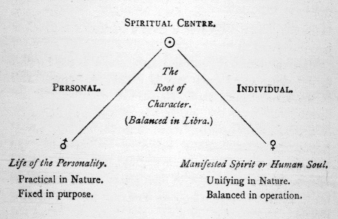

SPIRITUAL CENTRE.

The Root of Character.
(*Balanced in Libra.*)

PERSONAL.   INDIVIDUAL.

Life of the Personality.   *Manifested Spirit or Human Soul.*
Practical in Nature.   Unifying in Nature.
Fixed in purpose.   Balanced in operation.

Venus, the planet of the human soul, is in the seventh, the joy of Venus, and in her own sign, Libra. This is the house of the Individuality, and we can only come to one conclusion from the positions of Mars and Venus, and that is the fact that both Personality and Individuality are strong, giving a powerfully strong character.

And now for the Sun, the centre, or kernel, of the

character.   This is placed in the decanate of Venus in her own sign, giving all the gentleness of the Venus nature. The sign Libra gives, as described in Chapter XVI., a sensitive, compassionate, just, generous, inspirational, and perceptive nature.

In this way we have some idea how to judge of the Character, and by the foregoing diagram we may obtain a deeper insight still.

We must now consider the mind as the expression of the Character, purposely leaving out all consideration of Uranus for the present, to save confusion.   The mental rulers we have stated are the MOON, SATURN, and JUPITER, which in their totality are represented by *Mercury*.   The Moon we find is with Jupiter in Cancer, and Saturn is in Pisces, the Moon as the central point of the consciousness being in sympathy with both ($\delta \, \mathcal{U} \, \triangle \, \hbar$).   These three planets are in watery signs, thus indicating an emotional mind, the energies of which will be turned from the emotional into the devotional, as indicated by the conjunction of Moon and Jupiter.   This latter position gives a love of truth and a great desire for accuracy; first and foremost in the search for knowledge will be the truth seeker, and our intelligent subject will always endeavour to probe Nature's secrets in order to get at the *truth*.   The perfect harmony between these mental rulers will make the mind capable and competent, and everything will be brought to the mental standpoint.   We have seen that the temperament is the mental-emotional, which means that feeling will be blended with thinking.   She will *feel* truth. This feeling truth gives the very highest intuition, out of which pure wisdom must eventually come.

We will now analyze the mind from these planets,

making the following diagram for the purpose of easier study :—

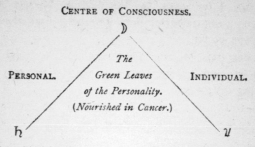

CENTRE OF CONSCIOUSNESS.

☽

PERSONAL.

The Green Leaves of the Personality. (Nourished in Cancer.)

INDIVIDUAL.

♄

♃

Crystallized Intellect.
The earth-life memory.
The concrete and personal element.
The brain-mind of the personality.

Preserved Memory of other lives.
Individual Consciousness.
Permanent storehouse of virtues.
The "kingdom of heaven."

Taking the Moon first, which is the Centre of the Consciousness of the earth-life, or the physical manifestation of that which is to be dissipated as FATE, we can arrive at some idea as to the life's mission. The Moon is the collector of the mist, or result of the contest between spirit and matter, and her position must represent what has to be reaped. She represents the fabric which has been woven on the loom of matter, and upon each appearance in the clothing of material flesh she is the garment of the mind—the outer garment,—the putting off of which requires conscious knowledge and individual ability.

The sign the Moon occupies, and the nature of the planets to the aspects of which she applies, indicate the work to be done ; for in every life we must *work* to become self-reliant, self-dependent, strong and wise. The planetary aspects from which the Moon separates are those relics of the past that lie in wait for us, the result of past accomplishments.   Here the Moon has separated from the trine of Saturn, square of Sun and Venus, and applies to the sextile of Mars, the square of Mercury and Uranus and the conjunction of Jupiter.

This produces a study in " cross-aspects "—which are always a puzzle to the student.   The Moon separates from the trine of Saturn, and square to the Sun; therefore, in a measure these two aspects balance each other, yet they will act in their own peculiar way.   The trine to Saturn will produce industry, stability, perseverance, patience.   It indicates harmony between the brain-mind, and that outside of it, the world-mind, so to speak, and will give a great love of justice, and a moral mind.   This has been earned in the past, brought over from previous lives.   The square to the Sun is now a matter of mind and spirit in conflict, the mind's rebellion against certain dictates of the spirit, producing changes, and an unrestful desire to experiment.   Mind and spirit are here crucified by each other.   It indicates many past conflicts between soul and spirit, the unity of which may take place about the thirty-fifth year of the present life, as a complete reading of the map indicates.

The next aspect is the separation from the square of Venus, another indication of war between character or spirit and mind.   This may be characterized as a conflict between the Human Soul and the Animal Consciousness. Both planets are angular and occupy their own houses, so that the contest promised is severe; but, like the others, it has been woven in the past, and needs this life to expiate it.   Many a thorny wound will come through this aspect, in which domestic life and ties will be sacrificed, for only through pain and suffering can the old consciousness be broken up. As a relic of the past, however, it will fade away, for mind must inevitably yield to spirit. Yet it will be hard to tear up the roots of the domestic home-life, and many a tear must be shed, for these are separations— in truth they are. Nevertheless, only by separating from the bonds of personal ties can we recognize our ties to a higher life, one in which the Individuality is bound to all, and favours none; for each must stand upon his own support, and fight his own battles to the end.

The applications are next in order for consideration. The Moon first applies to the sextile of Mars, indicating that courage, energy and endurance will be worked into the nature. It shows the harmony between the physical life and the mind, and that the personal character and the personal mind are harmonious, so that a fearless personality will be the result. The next aspect is the square to Mercury. In a measure this is the most unfortunate aspect. It gives the subject a far too critical brain, a tendency to doubt and criticize, a touch of sarcasm, and certain false preconceived notions, the result of which will be eventually to break up all conventionality. Much will have to be pulled down before the new can be built up; limitations and barriers will have to fall, and the very materialistic tendencies here denoted will have to be well weighed and sifted by the Mercurial mind. But it will offer the means to slay the lunar consciousness when the time is ripe. As Venus is mixing its influence with Mercury, in opposition to Uranus, great will be the crashes, and chain after chain will be broken, smash after smash will come, for, hung between the Mercurial and Uranian influence is the Moon, upon the cross of externals. There is no hope and no escape. The yearnings of the past have brought the soul in conflict with all physical connections.

There never was a better illustration of the truth of our wonderful science, as well as of the symbology of this aspect, than in the life of our subject, for it has been one that would move the strongest human emotions to their very depths. Of a verity, it is from war that she is now on her way to peace. Her previous life alone, to say nothing of the cause for which she has done so much, and which she so ably expounds, is sufficient to convince the most concrete intellect of her unfaltering love for truth; and well indeed may she desire no other epitaph than that "She tried to follow truth."

Who will deny the truth of the stars after an illustration like this, and who can doubt the value of the Wisdom Religion, which teaches us that we suffer from ourselves, that every living Soul has made his own Chart, and is making his future? For we reap what we have sown. If we yearn and aspire to be crucified on the cross, then shall we call down upon us all those old thought-forms which for ever cling to us until we seriously dispose of them by transmutation.

Here are facts, not theories. Every average man can test their truth. The method laid out in this work is simple and plain, and each reader may experiment with his or her own horoscope, and prove or disprove it. Some day this work must be done. Some day this aggregation of outgrown material must be swept away. *If not in this life, then in some other.* For if reincarnation is not true, if we do not inhabit fresh bodies to work off our past, then is all life a farce, and we come here to suffer for no useful purpose. The subject of this horoscope has suffered, and has suffered bitterly, as all the world is aware. But she has come through storm to peace, and has now realized the last aspect which the Moon applies to—the conjunction of Jupiter. Measure up how you will, you will find this is the last application of the Moon, and it means Peace. It is the final union of the Lower with the Higher Consciousness, the past worked off. The "kingdom of heaven within" is realized, and the homes of the Devas are found.

A second Pilgrim's Progress could be written from this truly Divine symbology, written in points of light across the skies, where selfish man cannot reach to alter or destroy. And in its pilgrimage every soul will some day come, as this glorious woman has, to peace and bliss. Her life has been one of service, and upon that cross she has sacrificed herself. Fame and honour have indeed been hers, and are her due. None could have suffered more in the search for truth and liberty, and her life is an example to all of what a human soul can do in the search for its celestial garment. She stands to-day as a living monument of what the future humanity may become, and her value will be appreciated only when the present vessel has been exchanged for a more glorified one

(b) Contrast Map, No. 6.

By contrast and comparison we may learn the qualities and properties or different forms of expression of what is the same spirit working through different vehicles. In the previous delineation we dealt with Aries upon the Ascendant, the signs rising in the natural order of the zodiac. The present horoscope, however, No. 6, has Libra on the Ascendant, thus reversing the order of the signs as regards their relation to the houses. This fact brings us to the important consideration of—environment.

As we have before mentioned, the twelve divisions called Houses describe the environment or surroundings into which the native is born. When the signs are distributed on the cusps of the houses in the order of the zodiac, that is, starting with Aries upon the Ascendant, and following on in due order—as is mainly the case in Horoscope No. 5—then the natural bent, the internal desires and inclinations of the native will be followed. It will be, as it were, the starting of the journey from the beginning, and the native will agreeably incline to the natural order of the planetary positions; the point to overcome in this case being just the planets themselves. But supposing the signs fall in reverse or irregular order, then the indications of the houses must be first overcome, next the natural order of the signs, and finally the planets.

We may arrange these in three classes. Class 1 may take up the Ascendant at any point of the zodiac, the sign rising being then the ruling sign. This will give rise to complications which from an exoteric standpoint it is difficult to explain.

But the idea may perhaps be followed by means of a very simple analogy. Let us think of London as Aries. Now supposing one is born in a village or country town, miles away from London, which call Cancer—let us say Manchester—and lived there until one was twenty-one. Manchester would represent the environment, it would be the "local London," as it were, and for those twenty-one years one would be more or less coloured by the customs and peculiarities of the Manchester people. Then, let us say, one leaves home, family, and friends to permanently reside in London. In time one would shake off the old environment and settle into the new; no longer a Cottonopolitan, one would become a Londoner, leaving Cancer, as it were, to commence afresh, but on a higher level, in Aries.

This rough illustration will serve to distinguish between the natural order of the signs and their order in the houses of any particular horoscope, and also to show how the latter must in time be changed for the former.

Now let us carry the idea farther. Suppose one outgrew the customs and thoughts of the London environment, and dared to think independently for oneself, that one broke away from all conventionality, accepted custom, ceremonial religion and form—in fact, struck out for oneself and followed the bent of one's own internal and higher or Individual promptings. This would correspond to coming under the influence of the *planetary positions*, apart from signs. In a word, one would have left the personality for the individuality—the real part of oneself. Lastly, supposing one decided to overcome even the limitation of all planetary influence, then one would seek to unify one's will with the Divine Will, and, rising above all planetary ruling, would stand free, no longer an Adept striving upward, but a Master, standing free both from all desire and all limitation. Thus it may be seen that to pass out of the three classes is to become truly liberated.

Now, in considering Map No. 6 we find the order of the signs reversed, Libra the seventh sign being upon the Ascendant, and Aries on the cusp of the seventh. Venus is the ruler, placed in the seventh house in Aries, the house of Mars. It will be as well to tabulate the contrast, picking up the details as we proceed.

MAP 5.

MARS, ruler, in *Taurus*, the 1st house, and second sign.

FIRST sign on cusp of Ascendant.

SUN, VENUS, and MERCURY in *Libra*, Air, in the 7th house.

JUPITER in *Cancer*, Water, in the 4th house.

SATURN in *Pisces*, Water, in the 12th house.

MOON in *Cancer*, Water, in the 4th house.

VENUS, despositor of Sun, in *Libra*, Air, in the 7th house.

JUPITER EXALTED.

MAP 6.

VENUS, ruler, in *Aries*, in the 7th house, and first sign.

SEVENTH sign on cusp of Ascendant.

SUN, VENUS, and MERCURY in *Aries*, Fire, in the 7th house.

JUPITER in *Taurus*, Earth, in the 8th house.

SATURN in *Cancer*, Water, in the 10th house.

MOON in *Capricorn*, Earth, in the 3rd house.

MARS, despositor of Sun, in *Sagittarius*, Fire, in the 2nd house.

SUN EXALTED.

We will first consider the environment as governed by the first house and its ruler, for this has often an important after-effect upon the life.

In Map No. 5 we have a happy early home-life, as indicated by the fourth house. The native, courageous yet gentle, compelled respect both in action and desire, while the sympathy between the native and her mother in this case was perfect. It was not until her marriage, which took place in her twentieth year, that the harmony of the home-life was disturbed. This brought the first glimpses of unhappiness; for marriage in this case was doomed to be a failure. With an active temperament, the map gives every indication of the native's ability to adapt herself to circumstances and surroundings, while maintaining at the same time a freedom and liberty the instinct for which is characteristic of the true child of Mars. If liberty is interfered

N

with, then freedom at any cost must be obtained. And to this end the aspects formed the means.

But in Map No. 6 the reverse is the case. The ruler of the first is in the seventh, not free, but bound by the square of Saturn. The ruler of the fourth, the home-life, is the cold Saturn, who is in elevation in Cancer, his fall, and in direct affliction with the physical and mental rulers. Here we have a Libran-vital temperament, soft and yielding, loving ease and comfort, which fears to be bold and to strike out a path for itself, but suffers the bondage of limitation to age and selfishness. The environment is strong and holds. The ruling planet is in a sign uncongenial to its nature, and the tendency is to live in the ideal world and not the practical. Like a caged wild animal, the life is being frittered away between, as it were, iron bars and leaden chains; while Mars is burning up the spirit and the soul with its fierce chafing, the leaden chains of Saturn bind the body captive to a home that has grown uncongenial, bitter, and galling. Never could there be a greater contrast than between these two souls in this struggle for freedom and liberty. In one case the ties were taken up in this life, and broken when they were found to hamper the soul; in the other, the native was born into the house of limitation, a life of bondage to an aged relative which has lasted nearly half the life. From a sense of duty, whether mistaken or otherwise, the native has ever feared to sever the tie. The angular position of Venus, the ruler, gave freedom within certain limits during the period of the infantile stage, but slowly and steadily the pressure of fear began to bind her down to the influence of one whose selfishness has seldom been equalled. It seems strange that submission to the subtle but strong, and at times even violent, tyranny of her relative should have lasted up to the present time, but such is the power of fear that she has considered it her duty to submit to worse treatment than that at one time meted out to ordinary slaves. But as all things must happen for the best, the fate of this subject has had its good side, for in bondage the soul has learned patience and endurance. The motive, though apparently good, has been the means of binding the chains tighter nevertheless. But for the moment we are not concerned as to whether the action is justifiable or not. We cannot interfere with the vital springs which set this fate in motion, and at best can only express an opinion as to the causes which gave rise to it.

These facts give a striking illustration of how the nativity affords us a complete web of destiny. In the one case the keynote has been truth and liberty, in the other fear and bondage.

So much for environment. Now let us pass on to the character, and the mind which expresses it. In Map No. 5 the sub-influence of the Ascendant is mostly positive, Solar-Mars, courage predominating; in No. 6 the sub-influence of the Ascendant is more negative, Saturn-Venus, giving fear as to results. Again, the martial colouring of the ruler affords a contrast in itself; but a martial ruler always denotes impulse, self-will, and perverseness, into which a large tinge of self is thrown. In Map No. 5 there is a balancing up; ideals are made practical, resource is had to means which give the finest expression, and the most is made of all opportunities. In Map No. 6, on the other hand, the shot is never worth the powder expended. The intentions are excellent, but the means lacking. The ideals are of the very highest, but ideals his fall, and so the plans and designs of the architect lie buried. The consciousness which should be worked up as mortar to build with is frozen into a caked mass in the house where the workman should be. For this life it is a matter of changing places; but there is Hope from that planet which signifies this quality. It indicates *waiting* for opportunity. Such it has always been. The life has been spent in *waiting*. It is another case of "If I had money, what I would do." Yet some day, sooner or later, the workman *must* work his way into the position of becoming master.

Such has been the nature of this life—it has built ideals which so far have not been carried out owing to lack of opportunity, while in the other case much good and useful work has been done, although many mistakes have been made. Both souls are seeking truth, but the lives of each have brought them along different paths to the same goal. One has found peace after much tribulation in service to humanity. The other will also find it in due time, for it is a desire of the Soul.

We may briefly contrast our two maps as follows:—

No. 5.	No. 6.
Balanced Power. ☉ *in* ♎	Impulsive Thought. ☿ ♈
Hopeful Mentality. ☽ ☌ ♃	Despondent Mentality. ☽ ♑
Giving Love of Truth and Liberty. ♄ ♓	Ever Recognizing Pain the Teacher. ♄ ♋
Balanced Soul. ♀ ♎	Impulsive Soul. ♀ ♈
Seeking Equilibrium. ☿ ♎	Seeking Ideality. ☉ ♈
Harmonious Tendencies. (Airy Signs.)	Spiritual Tendencies. (Fiery Signs.)
Seeking Devotion. ☽ ☌ ♃	Seeking Justice. ♄ M.C.

And now we will draw the veil over these contrasts.

There will be few who do not recognize these personalities. Their horoscopes are given so that all students may test the truth for themselves—and the truth none can deny. Much more could be written upon each, but sufficient has been said to illustrate the method of judging the life, mind, and character.

the serpent swallowing its tail. The line from the spiral motion has turned round upon itself; the "pairs of opposites" have re-united; positive and negative again are one, and in that centre of the great circle we have that which encompasses the whole and becomes compassion.

Thinking and feeling must become one. The two serpents which encompass the rod of Mercury typify the mind which is to become unified with the Divine Mind; the wings of thought must fly toward the highest consciousness.

Mercury or Hermes was the son of Jupiter and Maia, spirit and matter; born of the twain, he descends and ascends. This is the mystery of Mercury. He is the Divine Creative Wisdom. Venus was the daughter of Zeus and Dione, again spirit and matter. She was the goddess of love and beauty. When the fair son of thought adores the beautiful, and all thought is turned in the direction of love and beauty, then is there no longer duality, but unity.

In every symbol connected with Astrology this unity and duality is a marked feature, and must be understood before progress can be made. We realize ourselves by our opposites. We know spirit and life through its contact with matter. We realize the practical by living our ideals. To understand the planets we must understand ourselves. Saturn is the reaper and the sower; he is the highest and the lowest. As the husbandman who reaps he is the personal and physical manifestation of ourselves; his store is garnered up in Jupiter, the blessings of which are poured down upon us as the reward of abundant harvests. If we do not sow we cannot reap; and whatever may be the nature of our sowing, so will be the reaping.

Side by side in the Zodiac of positive and negative signs the duality of the planets is clearly marked, but in the circle which contains the whole is the unity. Soul and senses are one in Venus and Mars. They each find duality in houses opposite to their own. The end of the intellectual and maternal trinities we find governed by Mercury, reproduced as Jupiter in the opposite trinities. The light and the darkness may be seen in the Sun and Moon. It is all good and evil in duality, the unity of which contains neither.

For there is no good and there is no evil. All outside of the one self is illusion. Only in the heart of things can reality be found. To seek this, the personal self must be let go and we must live reality and become truth, love, and wisdom.

The maps that have been given will furnish a very good basis for the working out of these ideas by the student. But to bring home to himself the truths here set forth he should carefully cast and study *his own* nativity; for it is only when we apply our Astrology to the study and improvement of our own characters that it can truly be called Practical.

The first thing for the student to be sure about is the correctness of the *map*, of course, and if any hesitancy is felt about this it is well to have the nativity cast by some more experienced person in order to compare it with one's own efforts; for errors are very likely to creep in at first, owing more to unfamiliarity with the subject than to any real difficulty connected with it.

But the most important thing, as we have said so many times, is the *judgment*. And this the student should endeavour to develop for himself, along the lines we have indicated in this book. In order to help him still further we give a detailed reading of a nativity in a systematic way :—

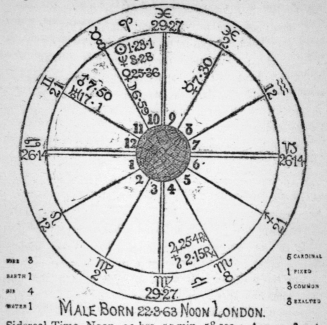

MALE BORN 22·3·63 NOON LONDON.

Sidereal Time, Noon, 23 hrs. 57 min. 58 sec. : Arc 359° 30′.

	DEC.		ASP.		
☉	1° N		☍ ♄ : ⚹ ♂		5 CARDINAL.
☽	16° N		⚹ ☿		1 FIXED.
☿	11° S		⚹ ☽ : □ ♂		3 COMMON.
♀	9° N		☍ ♃		
♂	23° N		□ ☿ : □ ♃		3 *Fire.*
♃	8° S		☍ ♀ : □ ☿		1 *Earth.*
♄	1° N		☍ ☉ : ☍ ♅		4 *Air.*
♅	23° N		P. ♂		1 *Water.*
♆	0° N		P. ☉ : ☌ ☉		
	Ascendant □ ♀ : □ ♃				Exalted : ☽ : ♄ : ☉

Ruler of the Nativity.—THE MOON.

This gentleman, who will be well known to many who read this, is a scholar of some renown; he has a University degree, and is the possessor of several titles. The horoscope is one in which there are several cross-aspects, which make it difficult for the student to readily understand. It will in itself, therefore, serve the purpose of illustrating a contrast, and the occasion also affords a means of giving a general reading of the nativity.

The method here adopted of reading the map is recommended as the best for the student to use in writing out his judgment. The reading under each heading should be extended beyond the brief condensation which we give, of course.

JUDGMENT UPON THE HOROSCOPE OF A GENTLEMAN BORN IN LONDON AT NOON ON 22ND MARCH 1863.

PREFACE.

This reading of the horoscope, according to the rules of the true Astrology, is given as an aid to the better understanding of the Personality, which is here in manifestation for the purpose of gaining experience for the soul or Higher Self, known as the Individuality.

The nativity indicates the progress of the soul, and clearly defines the one-life condition, which is the presentment of the lower quaternary, or Personal Self. During the manifestation of the Ego in the physical body, the WILL is free (within certain limits) to overcome the restrictions set upon it in former lives. The whole life history being as it were a book, this nativity is one of its pages. The past in the book has been written by the Ego, the future has yet to be written; but the next page is being written this life. The whole of the past and present fate is in this one nativity; but it may not all be expressed in actual life. To quicken our growth is to use up our past fate by calling it down upon us by our will. It is the WILL that is to finally overcome all planetary ruling. To strengthen the WILL is to free ourselves from physical limitations. To be free is to lessen the physical desires, for only when we have overcome and transmuted desire are we our own self-reliant selves.

INTRODUCTION.

At the time of birth the twenty-sixth degree and fourteenth minute of the fourth sign of the zodiac, Cancer, the sign of the Crab, and the sign allotted to the Moon, ascended. The lunar orb, which is the ruler of the nativity, is in her exaltation, in the sign Taurus, and dignified by her position in the midheaven. The greater light, the Sun, is also exalted and dignified by his position in the midheaven. The sign Aries is intercepted in the midheaven, and contains the Sun, Venus, and Neptune. Mercury is in the ninth house in Pisces, while Mars and Uranus are in the eleventh, in the sign Gemini. Jupiter and Saturn are in the fourth, in the sign Libra, the latter exalted there.

The majority of the planets are above the earth and in angles.

THE LIFE, CHARACTER. AND MIND.

The rising sign, Cancer, is feminine in nature. moist and receptive; ascending is the last portion of the third decanate, which is under the sub-influence of the planet Jupiter. This portion gives many good features, and the leading characteristics are shrewdness, activity, thought-fulness, and a nature at once high-spirited and contemplative. It indicates one who may be relied upon. It gives a very docile nature, one able to endure and display a considerable amount of both patience and persistence. The ruler is fixed in the firm and determined sign Taurus. in the portion governed by Venus, and aspected only by the sextile of Mercury. There are no planets in the Ascendant.

THE LIFE.

The tenacious nature of Cancer gives a strong hold upon life. The elevation of the ruler rising free from affliction argues a long life. The sign rules the breasts and stomach, which parts are liable to affection. There will also be a tendency to rheumatism and sciatica, as well as to absorb disease from others. The constitution is not of the strongest, and care at certain periods of the life will be needed to prevent sickness. Worry and anxiety will always produce ill-health.

The Sun, general ruler of the life-forces, claims the last twelve degrees of the first house, and seeing the exaltation of the Sun and its application to the sextile of Mars, the health will improve as the life advances. There will be a tendency to desire change, yet the life will become fixed, the sentiment of honour and duty doing much to influence the environment. Internal influences chiefly will mould the outer life, which will be noted for integrity, sincerity, and earnestness.

THE CHARACTER.

Cancer gives a somewhat reserved yet intuitive nature, pensive and introspective. Although discreet and independent, and very tenacious of purpose, there is an under-current of changeableness which makes those born under its influence difficult to understand at times. When fully under the lunar influence they are cautious, timid, distrustful, and even nervous, sensitive, and irritable. In this case the Taurean Moon will give a dogged perseverance which will ever point toward patience and endurance, the tendency ever being to hold on.

The SUN, as the centre of the Will, is martial in type, and its angular and elevated position will considerably strengthen the will and pull up all minor shortcomings. Dauntless courage is built into the Individuality; every failure will only add more and more determination to the spirit. The aspects of the Sun are to the opposition of Saturn (applying) and the sextile of Mars (applying). This forms a great contrast; but the Sun is in elevation, and can cope with the opposition of Saturn better than if below the earth. Both are in exaltation, and therefore strong. The true meaning of this aspect is spirit fighting intellect—another case of St. George and the Dragon; and St. George will win. But the fight will be long and severe, the combat being upon the external and practical side of existence, as shown by the cardinal signs and angular positions.

The *external* character, signified by MARS, will express itself through the mental sphere, and it will be the mental experiences that will delay the transmutation of Mars; yet it will be by this means that this lowest expression of the character will manifest. Mars is the Personal Will, and it is here engaged in mental wranglings which, although it will give great mental combativeness, will delay the progress; for the personality can only be convinced through the mind.

Between the Sun and Mars is the *internal* character-ruler, VENUS, planet of the human soul. This planet, we find, is also in elevation (placed above Mars, in fact) in the fiery sign Aries, the sign in which it can build its highest ideals — though ideals they often remain. Now the great drawback to this character-ruler is the opposition of Jupiter, though this is not quite so "St. George-like" in nature as the Sun opposition Saturn is; yet it is a great pull against this life's progress. Duality of a different nature between two benefics is here expressed; but out of this duality is to come final unity. It is Love and Devotion in twain, and not one. The external beauty is worshipped and the internal unseen. Justice is demanded and objective reason desired, rather than the internal Faith which questions not. It is a vital point, and shows the struggles of a soul with the external manifestation of things. The life-forces working through the brain (Υ) require the balance. Between Aries and Libra is the heart; into this the soul must retire and find the sacred heart of all things. Never was there a better illustration of a soul struggling for freedom.

The next point for us to consider is Character *versus* Mind.

THE MIND.

We have made it clear in which way the SUN, VENUS, and MARS rule the character, and we will now demonstrate how the MOON, SATURN, and JUPITER rule the mind.

The instinctual consciousness (MOON) is here fully alive, being free from hindrances and fixed for good in the decanate of Venus, applying very closely to the sextile of Mercury. The lower brain consciousness signified by the concrete SATURN is exalted in Libra, the airy and mental sign, but is below the earth and retrograde. Jupiter, representing the higher consciousness, is also retrograde in the sign of the balance.

The mind is essentially a strong one, refined and clear. It is concerned with the highest philosophy, but beyond the range of the mind it does not go. This internal mental nature is well shown by four planets in the airy or mental signs, and its external expression by five in cardinal signs. Fame will come through the mind. The native is noted for his mental acumen. In education and intelligence he has few equals. He is a lover of truth and justice, and in every possible manner answers to his horoscope.

The next point to consider is the planet Mercury, the synthesizing planet. Not only in a general way is it ruler of the mind, but in this case it rules the whole of the third or mind house. It is placed in the ninth, the house of philosophy, science, and religion, in the sign Pisces, the house of Jupiter. Pisces is the sign of understanding, and from its receptive nature, thoughts and ideas are readily received, either to be rejected or retained, as desired. The sextile to the Moon makes the latter receptive to the highest thought, while the square of Mars afflicts the mind by worry and anxiety, and gives a peculiar combative hardness, which wastes much of the mental force and energy over purely technical or academical points that are only needed by the conventional mind. The wise understand with their soul — they feel truth — while the mind argues and thinks, coldly, to know truth. But it is through the contest that the soul grows. It is only through meditation and contemplation that the mind

can be stilled, so that the calm, cool voice of the soul may be heard. This horoscope indicates a man of strong character but still stronger mind. When the personality, as expressed through the mind, is conquered, then will the fulness and beauty of the Individuality become manifest.

GENERAL READING.

The first three houses, while governing the life, character or soul, and mind, also indicate the environment, finance, and education, relatives, &c. The environment in this case was undoubtedly good, both from a social and financial standpoint, Moon ruler in Taurus free from affliction. He came from a military family. The finance is ruled by the Sun as ruler of the second house; also by Venus, general significator of wealth. Both are afflicted by oppositions. He gave up all he possessed to further the interest of the cause to which he attached himself, because of his splendid moral principles. His dauntless courage in this respect made of him a true hero. It may be judged that his relatives are not in agreement with his actions by the affliction of the ruler of the third with Mars, ruler of the fifth and depositor of the Sun.

Passing to the other houses, we may briefly sketch the outline of the life. The fourth governs the home and the end of affairs. The natural ruler of the fourth is upon the ascendant; owing to the square of Jupiter and Venus, both connected with the fourth house in this nativity, the natural home-life was broken up and a new home and environment made quite early. Still further changes are marked, and at the end of life it will have a tendency to become very unsettled. As it is, in the adopted home many changes may be expected, and the companionship of extreme persons is very plainly indicated. It is a home in which balance is necessary to endure the strain of the personalities and individualities which mingle there, indicated by Saturn and Jupiter in Libra.

The fifth house is ruled by Mars; the natural ruler is the Sun, which is the constructor and generator. Neither courtship, children, nor speculations trouble him upon the physical plane. He is a thought-father, and courts truth before the sexes; his speculations are all philosophical. The ruler of the fifth is in the third sign, therefore the energies of this house are mental and not physical.

The sixth, which is the house of sickness and magical phenomena, is governed by Jupiter, retrograde in Libra. Sickness will be produced by worry and mental strain. Ordinary magical phenomena he abhors, and he will not for a moment entertain the morbid psychic. His magic is the image-making power of thought and will.

The seventh is governed by Saturn, which afflicts the Sun from the natural ruler of the seventh, Libra. He is married to the sole purpose of uniting his lower self to the higher.*

The eighth house is governed by the mystic Aquarius. He is hardly to be called a mystic, though he believes in occultism—of the true occult; but he is too completely intellectual to express or realize the internal meaning of true occultism.

The ninth house expresses him admirably. He is a scholar, and the dual nature of Pisces indicates his work,

* The native has, however, married (since this delineation was first written) a highly intellectual and cultured woman, who has been of great assistance to him in his studies. He is something of a misogynist in his way, like many of the old philosophers, so that this may be termed an intellectual union.

which is the attempt to blend the scientific with the religious. This brings him the trouble, sorrow, and joy of his life. He is an editor, author, and translator; also a speaker. This is the most active part of his life, and Mercury in Pisces well expresses it.

The tenth house, ruling the moral qualities, contains the Sun, Venus, and the Moon. His moral character is beyond reproach. He holds an exalted position in life, and has won the respect and confidence of every one who has known him. His reality and thoroughness impress all who know him.

The eleventh house rules the hopes, wishes, desires, and friends or acquaintances. When he drops all personal ambition and mental combativeness, then he will touch the Uranian influence which waits the casting off of the last sheath. Then will the eighth house be fully expressed and the spiritual soul awaken. His friends are a mixture of Mars and Uranus. He alone knows the bitterness of the cup which he has drunk through the duality of his friends. The sign of the twins expresses a great crisis in his life, when the separation of the Martians from the Uranians among his friends took place.

The twelfth house is unoccupied. His self-undoing means his own undoing.

Such, in brief, are a few ideas upon which to judge the nativity. In later volumes we propose to go fully into detail regarding the meaning of the Twelve Houses * and the Natures of the Planets,† with special reference to the mystery planets Uranus and Neptune.

* *How to Judge a Nativity, Part I.* (7s. 6d.).
† *How to Judge a Nativity, Part II.* (7s. 6d.).
(The two bound together, 10s. 6d.)

CHAPTER XXI

HOW TO IMPROVE THE LIFE, MIND, AND CHARACTER

FROM stage to stage we have advanced in this simple method of instruction, until we now have at least three clear and definite ideas as to the best way of judging the life, mind, and character, astrologically, in each individual horoscope. Now the purpose of this work is to give the student the best means of making the study of Astrology thoroughly practical; and to this end it is intended to be a system by which he may profit through the study of himself, and thus overcome the lower fate and limited environment. To the indication of the best means of accomplishing this purpose, the present chapter will be devoted.

We have seen how the life is poured through the First House or Ascendant. This life is the primary physical consideration. It has its expression in the first house, corresponding to the sign Aries, of which Mars is the ruler; but its root and essence is in the Sun, the exaltation of which is the sign Aries. The physical Sun which we see in the heavens is the source of all life, light, and heat. The rays of the Sun are bright or dull in accord with the medium through which they pass. A bright and sunny day may be compared to the vital temperament and a cheerful Solar or Jupiterian disposition, while the same rays passing through leaden clouds correspond to a less life-giving temperament and a Saturnine nature. The same life in altered conditions will manifest differently, everything depending upon its mode of expression. It is the life that warms our senses on the physical rung of the ladder; it is the same life on the next step that stimulates the mind, and finally the same life is in our character. It is spirit in manifestation upon the material plane of existence; and it may be used wisely, or abused. If too much life is pouring through the senses and not under the proper control of the Ego, then its abuse by over-use of the senses is a danger to be guarded against; for one can live in the senses to the detriment of the mind and soul. The life pouring itself out through the senses may overrun them to such an extent as to end in abnormal sexual excess, which is the condition of those who are not under their own control. It may also find expression in anger and violence. When the senses are allowed full play, any external excitement may draw out the life. When ungoverned by a strong will all forms of passion arise from the crude and unrefined condition of this life-force. It has often been said "the greater the animal the greater the man," and so if this life-force is transmuted, controlled, and governed, then there is power, and the necessary energy to accomplish the desires of the soul.

From iron to steel and then to gold is the alchemical stairway that all must climb. Life is progress, life is earnest, life is real—and we must either refine our life or delay our evolution.

The zodiacal and planetary influences correspond to

the various colours that make up the spectrum. These colours can be seen in the "auras" of persons. The ascendant will in general give the clue to the predominant colour shown.

If our ascendant is a dark and muddy red, then we must purify our passions and desires until its colour becomes the rosy tint of warm love and gentleness. If the brown-grey tint of selfishness is aroused, then only by becoming more and more unselfish can we make our life such that it fulfils all that we expect of it. We have just so much life and no more; its energy may be conserved and used wisely, or wasted and spoilt, as we will. It is *knowledge* that will help us to avoid waste, and through the medium of the mind we can understand the life-forces thoroughly. The first step toward improving the life will be to study purity. Never until we begin to live clean and pure lives, can we make one step toward real progress. The senses must be purified if we would make any soul attainments. To be happy we must be pure; to be healthy we must be pure; and, before we can ever hope to become wise, WE MUST BE PURE.

The next consideration is the mind. The physical body needs life to sustain it. Every cell in the body has a consciousness of its own, but the crowning consciousness is the brain upon which the mind plays. This mind is the vehicle of the soul or the character. This is the most difficult of all to understand, for the mind to know itself must be analyzed by something higher than itself. The mind, however, cannot get beyond itself, therefore those who have not developed the *soul* state of consciousness, will never understand that there is something higher than the mind. But Astrology when treated by the soul, when *lived*, that is to say, makes clear the difference between itself and the mind. The third house rules the mind: its ruler is Mercury. This planet is convertible, and acts in accordance with the planet with which it is in aspect.

The symbol of Mercury is made up of all the planets, and has the three symbols in one. The mind is the great illusion, the snare and deceiver. Deluded by appearances, it takes the unreal for the real; ever changing, it is coloured by the passing objects or influence; swayed by desire, it clings to the senses for its most vivid sentient life. To overcome the mind is to partly overcome the stars, and therefore this is a most important study.

We specialize the rays of the Sun through a special organ in our body called the spleen. The altered condition of the Sun's rays becomes vitality; it is a force pouring downward. In the same way the mind is an elemental essence which is pouring down into manifestation, and as it passes through our brain, we specialize or educate it, moulding it by our will into the thought-forms which constitute the thought-action, leading finally to actions.

The Moon in a measure represents the lowest form of simple consciousness. But it is Saturn who marks off the definite condition of the lower physical brain-mind. It is this crystallized condition of mind which all must pass, the over-stepping of which means real progress. All crude and limited minds are held by Saturn, and none can pass into the plane of Mercury until Saturn is passed. To identify ourselves with our minds is to be under the sway of Saturn. The Saturnine mind is united to the brain organ, and can never leave the concrete or purely objective. The unfettered mind is shown by Mercury, which is expansive and adaptable to higher and advanced thought. Saturn and the Moon entirely govern the personality, or that which is limited to the material and physical. If linked to Mars, then the senses will hold the mind captive, that kind of experience being necessary for growth at that particular stage.

Now, how are we to improve the mind? We have tried to explain what the mind really is, but we must carry our ideas from this point still farther. What is it that thinks? The word mind is derived from Manas, the root of which is *man*, to think. The thinker is the true Man.

What *are* we, after all? We certainly are not our physical bodies, for these we leave when asleep. We certainly are not our minds, for these we can use in any given direction, making them obey the dictates of our wills. And to be wise we rule our minds, and thereby rule our stars. But how are we to accomplish this task? First, to improve the mind we must expand it beyond the limitation of Saturn; then, having expanded it, we must *control* it.

To control our minds is the secret. Thousands to-day are thinking other peoples' thoughts. Their minds are simply dust-bins for the refuse thought of others! Unable to deliberately do their own thinking, they drift into the ever-changing thought-currents of the day. The world's thought is one common thought in connection with the personality, which has never expanded outside of the brain consciousness. Nothing can be cognized that does not come within the range of the five senses. and all outside of them has no existence for their narrow vision. Such a study as Astrology could not be investigated, simply because the brain could not embrace so wide a subject. This is why advanced thought makes such little progress. Men *will not* think for themselves.

To improve the mind, we must expand it beyond the range of the physical into the metaphysical. To control the mind, we must think only of that which we choose to think. The mind must be our servant, and not our master. To improve it we must contemplate the beautiful, the ideal, and the real. We shall never know ourselves until we thoroughly understand our minds. But there is a simple means of doing this, just as there is a simple means of refining the body, by *purity*. The mind may be improved by seeking truth—to be ever truthful, ever loving truth before falsehood, ever seeking the true. It is the truth alone that must set us free. The mind is illusive and deceptive. Fear and worry are its torments and its hell. Let us seek truth, and we shall be free from snares and delusions. Let us watch our thoughts, and direct them into the channels which lead to the soul — that which is behind the mind—our REAL SELF.

And now to come to the final consideration of How to Improve the Character. The simplest word to use in connection with character is Soul. The use of this word simplifies the conveying of ideas astrologically, and in its human aspect it is represented by Venus. The character is governed by this planet and the second house, the central point of the intellectual trinity, between the first and third houses.

For the moment we will step outside of these three houses and consider the whole. The centre of each trinity represents the Soul, the whole coming under the fixed signs as follows:—TAURUS governs the human soul, LEO the spiritual soul, and SCORPIO the animal soul, while AQUARIUS stands for the Man in which all Souls are combined, the ruler of which is Uranus, the unbounded. The improvement of character means the growth of the soul. The withdrawal from the senses, the upturning of Mars, produces the human soul. The growth of the soul is by love and beauty, the artistic and the wonderful. Its magic power is will; its password, I will be what I WILL to be; and, when it *wills* to pass the limitation of the stars, then it is freed from the wheel of re-birth.

The growth of the soul is toward the eternal spirit. The final good of man is a spiritualized soul. We may improve and purify our senses, also educate and refine the mind, but it must be the work of the soul to prompt this transmutation. The soul must grow, the character must become more noble, firm, and self-reliant, until all the virtues are built into the permanent soul.

This, then, is the task before every Astrologer, and the whole of the human race. Astrology is but one of the seven keys to wisdom. Into your hands has now come this knowledge. How will you use it? It has opened one of the doors into the temple. Pass in through the silence of your own soul, and there in meditation realize that the ceaseless wheel of fate must ever turn for those who have not overcome the Personal Self. The secret of " He who loses his life shall find it," is here. The wheel can no longer turn for him who has the courage and the strength of will to stay the outgoing forces. Concentration of energy and mind toward the Divine is the end of the life's work. Then, when we have realized through the lesser Mysteries the glory of existence by sacrificing the lower to the higher, we shall come into the final initiation, which will give us the power to become the

"Wise Man Who Rules His Stars."

CHAPTER XXII

FINAL CONSIDERATIONS

THE sole aim and object of this work is to place before the world the true Astrology. No other work in existence has treated the subject in the same manner.

The fundamental principles of Astrology have ever been the same, and in no way have these principles been altered. The symbols have ever had the same internal meaning, and for the student whose eyes are metaphysically opened they reveal the progress of the soul from spirit into matter and back again into the spiritual world, after having added to itself as a quality the self-consciousness gained through the experience.

The student should endeavour to discover the true meaning of the planets and the signs before he attempts to blend them, and he should never forget that they are merely the symbols of forces through which the real life, or spirit, is manifesting. We are not matter, but spirit. Everything in the universe is Spirit, only in diversified conditions, and the nativity describes these conditions.

The best possible advice we can give the reader is that he first study his *own* horoscope thoroughly, so that he may become acquainted with himself, for until he knows himself he cannot know others. Never let him make the mistake of thinking that the personality is *himself;* he it is not. The real Ego is beyond the horoscope, and the highest point he can reach is the understanding of his own human soul. When he has gone beyond this, he will be an adept, and a new light will be thrown upon Astrology.

Never let him attempt to predict the future or dabble in what are called "directions" until he thoroughly understands the Radix, or the root, the horoscope of birth. The future lies in that, which is merely to become unfolded. If he is anxious to know *why* the planets affect us, he must endeavour to understand the re-embodiment of the soul, without which idea there is no sense or meaning in Astrology.

The planets affect us through the "elemental essence," which is life on its way downward, while we, on our way upward, have to contend with this essence, which expresses itself through the senses and the mind. The soul has to shake itself free from both. Mars represents the physical-animal senses, while Saturn represents the personal mind. If we overcome these two elements, progress is sure. The Moon indicates the line of fate, and the Sun that of destiny. If we follow the latter, freedom from illusion will be reached. We must always remember that we are in this life sowing for the next life's reaping; the sowing is our thinking, and therefore if we take care of our thoughts the acts will take care of themselves.

To the Reader: A Personal Note.

To become a good student you *must* have concentration and become devoted to the study. If the subject is worthy of your study, then it is worth doing well. The advantages will become apparent as you advance.

Do not attempt to give a reading of any nativity until you can give a complete and correct judgment without reference to this or any other book. Master the theoretical part of the science before you attempt the practical. However short and tentative may be the delineation you attempt, *do it all without consulting any "authority"*: only in this way can you learn to rely upon yourself.

Always bear in mind that although all that is published concerning Astrology belongs to the Lesser Mysteries, there is a religious and sacred side to this science, as well as a practical one. The shell can never have the same value as the kernel; therefore, seek the *internal* meaning. The purer your life, the clearer will become your prophecy.

If you abuse your admission to the truths set forth in this work, the gate of knowledge for you will shut completely this life. If you use them wisely, it will lead you to wisdom.

THE END

WHAT IS A HOROSCOPE AND HOW IS IT CAST?

Third Edition.   **2/-, post free 2/2.**

An elementary work on Astrology. It fully explains the meaning of a horoscope in all senses of the word, and is entirely free from calculations of any description.

THE HOROSCOPE IN DETAIL.   *Fourth Edition.*

2/6, post free 2/8.

A Complete Supplement to *What is a Horoscope and How is it Cast?* giving all the additional details necessary for the study of the horoscope.

DIRECTIONS AND DIRECTING.   **2/-, post free 2/2.**

An introduction to predictive Astrology, dealing with King George's Nativity and Directions.

The "REASON WHY" IN ASTROLOGY.   *Second Edition.*

2/-, post free 2/2.

A philosophical treatise on Astrology. It is a very interesting Manual, full of suggestive and illuminating ideas.

MEDICAL ASTROLOGY.   *Second Edition.*   **2/-, post free 2/2**

A new and entirely original work. It is a valuable addition to this series of Manuals, dealing with the medical side of Astrology in a thoroughly efficient manner.

HORARY ASTROLOGY.   *Second Edition.*   **2/6, post free 2/8.**

This Manual explains the art of divination by Horary Astrology. It gives rules for obtaining the answers to questions such as :—*Will it be advisable to remove?* etc., etc. It contains a complete Glossary of Astrological Terms, an exceedingly useful addition.

THE DEGREES OF THE ZODIAC SYMBOLISED.

Third Edition.   **2/6, post free 2/8.**

Every degree of the Zodiac is symbolised, and explained, by two distinct systems.

A THOUSAND AND ONE NOTABLE NATIVITIES.

Second Edition.   **2/-, post free 2/2.**

The Horoscopes of remarkable people, obtained from authentic sources. This is *the* book for students in search of horoscopes for study or reference.

MUNDANE ASTROLOGY :—National Astrology.

2/-, post free 2/2.

WEATHER PREDICTING :—Rules for judging the weather.

2/-, post free 2/2.

SYMBOLISM AND ASTROLOGY.   **1/6, post free 1/8.**

An introduction to Esoteric Astrology through Symbolism.

N.B.—All these manuals teach *practical* Astrology.

Practical Astrology.

Had this book been termed *Astrology in a Nutshell* it would have received an appropriate title. It is Alan Leo's first book on Astrology, written with fire and enthusiasm, and contains very useful, concise, and instructive lessons on Natal Astrology.

Price 5/-

Rays of Truth.

This book is the best to give to children, and those who wish to absorb the truths of Astrology without study. It contains a series of short articles written in a charming manner in which some of the deepest problems of life are treated in a way that none can fail to understand. We recommend this book to all who find study difficult.

Price 5/-

Astrological Essays.

A series of excellent essays dealing with Astrology from a philosophical aspect. It is written by Mrs. Bessie Leo expressly for the uninitiated who wish to know all they can about Astrology without study. It contains a photograph of Mrs. Leo.

Price 5/-

ORDER THROUGH YOUR BOOKSELLER

or from

Modern Astrology Office, Imperial Buildings, Ludgate Circus, London, E.C.